GET UNCOMFORTABLE
or CHANGE COURSE

UNDERSTANDING
WHAT IT TAKES TO BE
AN ENTREPRENEUR

Kelvin G. Abrams

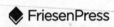 FriesenPress

One Printers Way
Altona, MB R0G 0B0
Canada

www.friesenpress.com

ISBN
978-1-03-918264-6 (Hardcover)
978-1-03-918263-9 (Paperback)
978-1-03-918265-3 (eBook)

1. Business & Economics, Entrepreneurship

Distributed to the trade by The Ingram Book Company

Dedication

I dedicate this book to all the future entrepreneurs.

Table of Contents

Introduction
Get Ready to Work

You are excited. You are driven. You are passionate. You have a dream. Most importantly, you are ready to stop talking and start doing!

I hear you. I have been exactly where you are right now. Soaking in as much knowledge as you can. Making big plans. Seeking resources. You think you know what it will take. You think you have it all figured out. I thought I did too! Let me tell you, I did not!

When someone tells you that you will make sacrifices, it does not phase you. Does this sound right? You think you are ready to give up a little extra time with your family, that you may work a few late nights, or that you might have to ask everyone to work around your schedule for a while until you can hire more staff. Sure, in theory this does not sound too bad. In practice this is not the experience of a small business owner.

You will miss important family functions. You will lose sleep. You will experience the kind of stress only financial insecurity brings. Your friends will get angry with you for not being around. Your significant other, if you have one, might try their best to be supportive, but at some point they will resent the time they lose with you. And dating? Well, that is a story for another book!

Starting your own business will test your strength in all areas of your life. It will push you to the brink in ways you never thought possible. Consider this book both a dose of tough love and your loudest cheerleader. I come to you not as a guru or an expert or a millionaire. I come to you with a strong desire to help you understand what it takes to be an entrepreneur. I don't want you to make the mistakes that I have.

I love it when people succeed. I want your business to work. I want you to realize your dream, but I firmly believe that you need to know what it will be like before you start. You need to have a clear picture of how your incredible dream will impact your life in every way so that it doesn't blindside you.

There are so many people out there selling the idea that being an entrepreneur is easy. They are experts on it. They tell you that you can make unlimited wealth through little work. Maybe you can. Maybe they did. Maybe it can be easy.

In my experience, over the last fifteen years living the life of an entrepreneur who now owns multiple businesses, I have never met one of these people in person. Every single entrepreneur I have met has either survived the roller-coaster of their life by hanging on tooth and nail, or they've been flung off, left to pick themselves up and try again or move on.

Does this scare you? It should. If you are afraid to be uncomfortable, you should change course! Read that last sentence again and let it sink in. Some people are born entrepreneurs. It is in their DNA. When the going gets tough, they do what it takes to keep going because there is no other option. They live each day of their entrepreneurial journey feeling uncomfortable, and if they don't feel uncomfortable, they know it's time to grow.

How do I know this? Because I am one. I was born an entrepreneur. It is in my DNA. From a very young age I found creative new ways to make money. When I was a kid I loved candy, and at the time (I'm about to age myself), I could get so much candy for a quarter. The problem was that extra quarters were hard to come by in my family. One day my brother and I had this idea that we would start our Window Toy Sale business.

The business plan was simple and effective. We opened our bedroom window and sold some of our toys to friends in the neighborhood until we made enough to get all the candy we wanted. Some of my personal favorites were those straws where you would cut off the ends and pour pure sugar straight onto your tongue, or Pop Rocks, those fun candies that exploded in your mouth. Candy was a great motivator!

I began seeing business opportunities everywhere. Another fun memory from my childhood that makes me laugh every single time I think about it was selling my cousin's autograph. Willie (Scottie) Scott was older than me and already in the NFL at the time. One day he asked me how much I got for one of his signatures. I proudly reported that I had sold one for fifty cents.

"What?! That's it?!"

The Work You Will Do

This book is all about doing the work! It's time to stop talking about what you plan on doing. It's time to actually do it. Some of the work you will do while reading this book is:

1. You will begin to understand that being an entrepreneur means getting creative every single day.

2. You will dive into your current mindset to understand if you were born an entrepreneur.

3. You will learn about banks and how to approach them for a business loan.

4. You will begin to create your business plan.

5. You will learn how to navigate some of the unexpected things life will throw your way with greater ease.

6. You will dream big!

7. Finally, you will get uncomfortable or change course.

Let's Walk Together

I think by now, even though we are only a few pages in, you are getting the picture. If you are feeling uncomfortable and you don't like it, maybe you want to change course, or maybe you want to keep reading. Maybe you want to arm yourself with as many tools as you can so that you don't make all the mistakes I did. If so, this book is for you! Let's take a walk down this entrepreneurial path together.

In the rest of this book, you can expect much of the same honesty you've experienced in this chapter. As you are reading, I want you to feel what it's like to walk in my shoes. In a way, I want you to come away from this book like you've got the experience of a person who has successfully thrived, and sometimes barely survived, in fifteen years of business. This book is meant to help you.

In your business you will work harder than you have ever worked before. You will work longer than you ever thought you could. And you will feel pain in places you never could have imagined. If you can deal with this, keep reading. If not, change course. Your journey might be extremely difficult, but it will be rewarding in the end.

I will share with you what I have learned about setting yourself up for financial success, some of the unexpected things that you can expect to happen, how to get creative, the ups and downs of having employees (especially in a post-pandemic world), ways that you can help alleviate stress, why it's important to reinvent yourself, and so much more.

Oh yeah, and there is one super important lesson I have not talked about yet: be prepared to laugh at yourself. Yes, you are serious about your business and yes, you are taking it seriously, but sometimes you gotta let go and laugh. In the spirit of laughter, I want to share a little entrepreneurial humor from my good friend Uncle Willie:

I love being self-employed, but my boss is a jerk!

Okay…are you ready to take a leap? Let's take a walk together!

Chapter 1
Born To Be An Entrepreneur
A Little About Me

My Dog Tiki

Throughout my life I have had many business ideas. I am happy to report that they have grown a bit more complex than the Window Toy Sales or selling of my famous cousin's signature. While completing my degree at Rutgers, I developed a business plan for a doggie daycare. It was really good. I loved the idea, but after graduating I did what a lot of graduates do: I got a job. My job was with the government and I liked it…at first. I made good money. I was stimulated. I had security.

But there was always something sitting in my subconscious pulling at my contentment. I had let the notion of what I was supposed to do in this life get in the way of what I thought I should do. I had stifled the creative entrepreneur for the sure thing, the safe bet, the comfortable way out. And deep down I really was not okay with it. I wanted more. I knew I could do more, but more important than that I knew I was ignoring my purpose. I was born to create!

It wasn't until I lost my sweet puppy Tiki, a cuter-than-cute Weimaraner, that I woke up. I loved Tiki from the moment I set eyes on him. He made life instantly better in the way only dogs can. Tiki was just eleven months old when I arrived home from work one day to find him paralyzed. He had experienced spinal-cord bleeding from a previously undiagnosed ailment.

At this heart-wrenching moment, when I had to say *goodbye* to Tiki far too soon, I knew that life had changed as I knew it. Things needed to be different. Tiki had spent much of his short life in a crate while I worked long hours at the office. It hurt me to think that I was not able to bring him more joy. This life-changing moment brought me back to my purpose. Tiki's death reignited my passion. He reminded me of that business plan I created back in college, and most importantly he inspired me to create a better life for other dogs while their owners were away from home.

Since 2008, Tiki's Playhouse has been my reality, for better or worse! I do have to tell you that the thing I am most proud of is what I have created for all the dogs that come to stay with us. I, along with some very caring staff, have made a place for dogs to play, socialize, and enjoy life while their humans are away. The dogs are a huge reason why I do what I do. Making sure they are cared for and kept safe is more important to me than the money, and I think this last point is also an important aspect for new entrepreneurs to understand.

When you love what you do and do it with integrity, it feels good, and when your work feels good, you will work even harder to make sure you are doing the best you can. This drive to do your best will ensure you create a standard for your business that your customers will recognize and appreciate. For me this means ensuring the safety of all our dogs at all costs. I do this by not accepting more aggressive dogs or taking on too many dogs. Does this mean I lose money? Yes. Does it make some people angry with me? Absolutely. But I will not compromise on the quality of the service I provide.

Getting up in the morning and knowing that no matter how hard my day might be, I have made a difference in the lives of both dogs and humans. That is why I do what I do. With unwavering determination, I strive to stay true to myself and my dreams. Am I perfect? Of course not. But I do the best I can.

I give back whenever I can, and sometimes even when I can't. This means doing things like lending a client your car to drive home to get an extra set of keys to their car because their sweet pup had locked them out and was stuck inside.

It also means sacrificing yourself in ways you may not imagine when you start your business. There have been many times since starting Tiki's Playhouse that the universe has given me the opportunity to go above and beyond. I think one of the most heartbreaking moments was when I had to stay with a dog in the final moments of her life because her family couldn't get back in time. They had just boarded a flight to Florida for a much-needed family vacation when I noticed their older dog was having breathing issues.

I immediately called the local vet, and she advised that I bring the dog in right away. Over the phone, the family decided that the best thing for their dog was euthanization. My client called me crying and asked if I could stay with their family pet so that she wasn't alone. It goes without saying, I would have done this without being asked.

I quickly ran across the street to a friend's restaurant and ordered a steak dinner. I then went back to the daycare and got their other dog and brought him to have a delicious last supper with his buddy.

I don't tell these stories for you to think: "Oh look at that Kelvin guy. He's such a good person!"

No, I tell you this to give you a clearer picture of what it truly means to be an entrepreneur with heart. One who, regardless of what they had planned to get done that day, would do anything for the people—or in my case, the animals—that they serve. This is the entrepreneur I strive to be. I know that if I no longer have the capacity to give of myself in this way when I know it's right, I will redirect and choose a new path.

Heart & Strength

When I reflect on my life and who I have become, I know it has a lot to do with my dad. He was always working. He was an entrepreneur as well, and sometimes things were tough. There were times when he would get up to go to work before we woke up and got home well after we had already gone to bed. I remember occasions when we would go weeks without seeing him.

This did not mean he slacked on disciplining us boys or left everything to my mom. There were three of us, and boy we could cause some trouble! And did we ever get in trouble for it! My mother often left the disciplining to my dad, probably because he was good at it. Even if he worked until the early hours of morning, he would check to make sure we had done our chores and our homework.

Imagine being deep asleep, and having been so for hours, only to have your bedroom light unceremoniously turned on.

"DAADDD!"

"KELVIN! There are dishes in the sink. You know the rules."

I would groan and try to cover my face. I knew it was useless to complain, but no part of me wanted to get out of my cozy bed. I instantly regret the moment I thought that maybe he wouldn't look in the sink when he got home.

"I promise I'll do them in the morning."

"No, you will not. You will do them now."

My dad would also rip the covers off our beds to wake us up.

I would drag my tired, half-asleep body out of bed and promise I'd never do this to myself again…until the next time!

The same went for homework. It did not matter how tired he was, Dad checked! If we weren't done or he was not happy with the effort we had put in, our tired, half-asleep bodies were being called back down to the kitchen table. Even though he had worked for almost twenty-four hours, he made sure we did the homework right!

We all hated it at the time. We wished he would just give us a break. We talked about our friends who had dads that weren't so strict. But in the end, I am grateful to my dad for the work ethic he instilled not only in me, but also in my brothers.

He led by example, and he held us boys to account. The greatest gift a parent can give their child is to care. My dad cared, and that is a big reason why I am who I am today. I am a mix of his work ethic, his dedication, and my mom's tough love.

That said, our family struggled with my dad's choice to open his own business. My mom was not always supportive. There were all of the sacrifices and worries that came with his choice like financial insecurity, her having to make up for what he couldn't do at home, and losing precious time with him. We all felt that it was a burden we were forced to bear without having given our consent.

I Will Thrive

You might be wondering why I would follow in my father's footsteps after having had such a difficult experience growing up. My simple response is that I have to. I have no other choice. I was born to be an entrepreneur. It is in my blood. I think my dad saw this in me, and this is why he pushed so hard. He wanted me to do better than he had. He didn't want me to see the things he saw as a black man growing up in the south. He wanted so much for his children.

I know things have been better for me than for my dad, but I do experience racism in my business. It is a challenge I can no longer tolerate or accept. No matter where you come from or how you look, if you see it happening do not just stand by. Say something, do something. It should be shocking to me that it happens, but sadly it isn't. Maybe one day it will be.

As much as I hate it, I have to accept the racism that is alive and thriving in America in my own way. As a business owner, I push my feelings aside because the business comes first no matter how I feel. Racism wins to a degree as a minority business owner. If I did not let it, if I spoke out against it, I would be labeled a difficult black man. This is a lesson I've had to learn, and so now sometimes I have to stay quiet when I just want to lash out.

I know there are people who will not leave their dogs at my daycare, come into my coffee shop, or buy a membership at my gym because I am a black man. I've seen people walk in and take one look at me and walk out. On one very memorable occasion, my employee, a white woman, and I made a house call to check on the temperament of a dog for a potential client. The client, a gentleman, had called and spoke with me on the phone before I arrived. I guess my voice didn't sound black. In fact, I get this all the time: "you sound white on the phone." I always respond by saying: "I guess my Rutgers education paid off."

Anyhow, as soon as the man opened the front door and saw me, I knew. He wouldn't acknowledge my outstretched hand. He would not even speak to me. He looked at me with pure hatred. His wife stepped in at times to speak with and acknowledge me. As we drove away, I noticed him looking around his property to see if anything was missing.

When this happens, I call on my inner strength and resilience. I remember my dad and all that he taught me when I was growing up. He pushed because he knew I could do better. He pushed because he knew I could make a real change in this world. Here I am. A multiple business owner. I am proud to be the face of my business. I am proud of who I am. I will continue to lead by example. I will continue to show anyone who does not think a black man or woman could or should run their own thriving business what my success looks like.

Heart.
Strength.
Resilience!

These are qualities I saw in my dad, and now they are qualities I see in myself. This is my legacy.

A Lonely Journey

Another tough lesson that my dad tried to warn me about was the loneliness I would experience. When you are an entrepreneur, you truly walk the path alone. There may be some loved ones, friends, or mentors who might join you for brief moments, but in the end it is all you.

When I told my dad about my plan to open Tiki's Playhouse, I remember his response as if it were yesterday:

"Son, your mom won't understand, your brothers won't understand. Your friends won't understand. It doesn't mean they don't love you or support you. They simply won't understand your journey."

He wasn't wrong. I thought things might be different for me than they were for him, but they weren't. I was the most hurt when I began to lose support from my family. In the beginning they were there cheering me on, but over the years it slowly changed. When you stop showing up to family events, they learn not to expect you, but it doesn't mean that they like it.

If you do not know this already: YOUR FAMILY WILL BE YOUR TOUGHEST CRITICS!

Let that sink in! You may have been raised to believe you will be loved no matter what, and that might make you think your family will then support what you do because they love you. Think again! Not about the being loved part, that may be true, but that does not mean they will support you and your business. Does that sound harsh? Probably. Remember, I am here to share the good, the bad, and the absolutely terrifying. Why? Because it is the truth that will keep you standing in the end.

Remember, this journey is yours, not your family's, your friends', or your girlfriend's. YOURS! Imagine walking in the woods. It's dark. There is nothing but trees in front of you. Somehow, someway, you have to get to the other side of that forest. The trees are your obstacles. Obstacles only you must overcome.

In some cases, your family will be your toughest critics simply because they love you and they are worried. Try to remember this through the hurt. They are human too. They have their dreams and desires. They will not understand why you choose your work over a family function. You might be accused of choosing your business over your family. The truth is that sometimes you will have to. What are you supposed to do, leave five dogs without care because your employee did not show up on Mother's Day? You will need to make tough choices, and sometimes your family will not understand.

There will also be times when you feel like you can't talk to anyone. Your business feels like it is failing and you know there is a solution. There is a missing piece to the puzzle. If you could just find it, everything would snap back into place. But you know that if you bring it up with your well-meaning but very pragmatic family or friends, that they will all say one thing: It's time to throw in the towel! But, like Edgar A. Guest said in his poem *Don't Quit*: "So stick to the fight when you're hardest hit. It's when things seem worst that you must not quit."

Also, when you have to make a tough decision, your mentor will offer advice, but ultimately you are the one who has to make the final call because you are the one who will suffer the consequences. The weight of your work cannot be shared. It is yours and yours alone.

This is the lonely part. I have sat up so many nights just thinking on my own, feeling absolutely and entirely alone in the world. I've cried. I've cried because I'm frustrated. I've cried because I feel I can't possibly give anything more. And then I get up the next day, and I keep working. Psalm 30:5: "Weeping may endure for a night, but joy cometh in the morning."

A huge part of the reason why I keep pushing is for myself. Without a doubt, I know this is my path, but there is a part of me that keeps on going to prove those who said I couldn't do it wrong. Like the girlfriend who dumped me two months after I started my business. Or the friend who said my business would fail. I want them to see that I did it! To all the naysayers — I DID IT! Fifteen years in business, enough lessons learned to fill a hundred books, and some battle wounds, but I am still standing.

In a way I hope this book is the person you can turn to in the middle of the night. Know that even though you feel so lonely in this moment, you are not alone. I understand your desire to succeed, but most importantly I understand why you keep fighting: It's because you have to. The path you know you must walk in this life is the one of an entrepreneur.

Quick Recap

1. Love what you do and you'll always do it with integrity.

2. Understand what your strengths are and how you developed them.

3. Get comfortable with your thoughts, the entrepreneurial journey can be a lonely one.

4. OWN YOUR STORY!

Chapter 2
Stop Talking, Start Doing
How To Take Action

"Discipline is a wonderful elixir for a culture desperately
seeking depth and purpose amidst the enfranchisement
of superficiality. In other words, ours is an age that would
rather feel disciplined than actually be disciplined."

—Rick Rigsby[1]

I remember exactly where I was when I decided to start working on a doggie daycare business plan. I was on a lunch break while on shift in the fitness center at the Marriott. It was one of my many jobs. I was exhausted. I was depressed. I was tired of working for people who treated me badly. I was tired of bosses that took advantage of me. I was just plain tired.

As I looked up at the sunny sky, I wrote this short poem—or sonnet or whatever it is you might call it—in my head:

Here I lay confused.
Here I lay battered, but not bruised.
Here I lay, what to do?
Here I lay defused.

---

1   Rigsby, Rick. *Third Grade Dropout: How the Timeless Wisdom of One Man Can Impact an Entire Generation*. Nashville Tennessee: W Publishing, 2006.

It was at this moment that I knew I would be my own boss one day. I would not allow myself to live a whole lifetime feeling the way I was feeling. I started to think about what I loved and what I could create a business for. My thoughts immediately went to dogs. I have always loved them. Well, dogs and the New York Giants, but I knew I had missed the boat on becoming a pro football player, so my early decision was to do something with dogs.

Once I got an idea in my head and it stuck, I went for it. I started reading magazines for entrepreneurs. I was looking to learn about the latest trends and was excited to learn that the dog daycare business was blowing up on the West Coast. I started learning everything I could. I even got a part time job at a dog kennel. I did not last long there. I realized very quickly that I didn't like the concept of a kennel. I hated all the barking dogs and the loud echoing noise against the cement walls. And the smell was horrible.

How could anyone who truly loved dogs create an environment like that for them? No, that was not how the dogs who came to stay with me would be cared for. They would have space to play. They would feel safe socializing with the other dogs. It would be a business, but it would also be something that was built with kindness and love. This is what I was talking a little bit about in the first chapter. Yes, people can make money. But the entrepreneurs who inspire me the most are the ones who create something great and put this first, even over profit.

As my frustration turned to daydreaming in the back parking lot of the Marriott, I may not have completely realized it, but Tiki's Playhouse had been born. But it wasn't until I lost my beloved dog Tiki and decided to devote my life to honoring his memory that it would come to life. Sometimes it takes a wake-up call, as tragic as this one was for me, to turn your talking into action.

I have to stop for a minute and share a funny anecdote with you. So, as you also already know, I LOVE the New York Giants. If you know anything about them too, you know where the name Tiki came from. In fact, all my dogs have been named after NY Giants football legends like L.T. (Lawrence Taylor), Carson (Harry Carson), Banks (Carl Banks), Strahan (Michael Strahan), and Tiki (Tiki Barber). Call me a fanatic but I bleed Big Blue!

Okay, back to Tiki. I don't think I captured in that first chapter just how devastated I was when I had to make the decision to end his life. I have never cried so much or so hard, and believe me, I have cried! Tiki was such an energetic dog during his short eleven months, three weeks, and three days of life. If you have ever had a dog, you know how much love you develop for them instantly. It still haunts me to this day that I had to put him down.

I didn't have enough money to continue with the type of care he would have needed. I was told he was completely paralyzed, and even if I could support his condition financially, it was not a good quality of life for a dog.

It simply broke my heart. I stopped eating. I cried more. I even called in sick to work for a couple of days because I could not get myself there. Sitting on my couch mourning the loss of my amazing pup was my wake-up call. It was time to stop talking and start doing. This life is short. I knew I was meant for more. Tiki reminded me of that.

Immerse Yourself

Once I made the decision, I went for it. I did this by arming myself with as much knowledge as possible. If you are going to do something and succeed, you can't jump in blindly. Read as much as you can. Take courses. Seek mentors.

I immersed myself in learning for several months. I bought books on both business and dog daycares. I learned everything I could about creating a successful business plan. I remember there being nights when I would wake up and have to work on both my business plan and my three-year pro forma plan because my brain would not stop thinking about it.

Once I thought I had a solid business plan, I took it to an organization called SCORE, a not-for-profit organization that provides free mentorship and resources to small businesses. There are chapters throughout the country and all their mentors are volunteers. In their own words: "SCORE's mission is to foster vibrant small business communities through mentoring and education. We aim to give every person the support they need to thrive as a small business owner."[2]

If you don't have a SCORE in your country, I would do some research to see if there is an equivalent organization. I cannot recommend this service enough. You are paired with entrepreneurs who want to see you succeed. They care!

My mentor was Ed Knox. Boy, was he tough. I mean tough! I remember bringing in a color presentation of my business plan and being so proud of it. I thought that I had done my homework. HOLY COW BATMAN, I was wrong!

Ed tore my business plan apart. He reminded me of my expository writing professor at Rutgers. Red writing over the entire thing. Talk about being crushed. I wanted to quit. In fact, I did. It took me a couple of weeks before I made another appointment with Ed. He tore my plan apart again and politely said, "don't waste time presenting a colorful professional business plan, we have a lot of work to do."

With that said, I got to work.

The next time I went back, I thought I had done my homework. I was proud of myself but knew more of what to expect this time. I was getting used to Ed being tough on me.

"Good morning, Kelvin. I assume you're ready for me?"

"I don't know if I'm ever ready for you Ed," I joked, "But yes, I have done my best to address your notes from our last visit."

"Good. Let's get to work."

I took a deep breath, sat down, and prepared myself for Ed's feedback.

"Today we are going to dissect your business plan piece by piece. I want to really look at your projections."

---

2   https://www.score.org/content/mission-vision-and-values

"Okay."

"First of all, do you see this number right here?"

"I do."

"Can you explain to me how you came to it?"

"I did some research on what kinds of expenses to expect with a dog daycare and this is the average that I was told to expect."

"That's not good enough. You need to get more specific. More work needs to be done here."

I gritted my teeth and made a note, even though I wasn't even sure where to start.

"Now, where are the expenses for the admin side of the business?"

"What do you mean?"

"Things like pens and paper."

This was just the beginning. As a first-time business hopeful, I was unaware of all the expenses associated with running a business. I missed a lot of things.

Each meeting after this one involved looking at the financials and adding additional expenses. It was like Ed was testing me. *"Let's see if I can break this guy by throwing curve balls."*

Of course, Ed had my best interest at heart, but some days it sure didn't feel like it. The most frustrating part of the process was thinking I had done my homework correctly, only to have Ed completely destroy it in front of me.

Several times, I confronted Ed, "I did everything you asked."

"You did. It's not there yet."

What I didn't realize was that Ed was teaching me how to overcome obstacles. I re-worked and re-worked my finances at least ten times or more. Finally, I realized I was outmatched by Ed's wisdom and knowledge. This is when I decided to hire my CPA.

I have to admit to you that I hate numbers. I am not a math guy at all. Creativity is one of my superpowers, so having to fight with numbers did make me hate life a little. For this reason, I decided to hire a CPA to help with my business plan. This is a good point to highlight: DON'T EXPECT YOURSELF TO BE AN EXPERT AT EVERYTHING.

Lean into your strengths. Like I said, I am creative. I can create a new idea for a business in my sleep. I am also determined and resilient. These are the strengths I lean into, for anything else I get help.

Just in case you do not know: CPA stands for Certified Public Accountant. The CPA license is provided by the Board of Accountancy for each state. There are equivalents to CPAs in other countries, most notably Chartered Accountants.

Why would you consider hiring a CPA over a CA?

"Not all accountants are CPAs. Those who earn the CPA credential distinguish themselves by signaling dedication, knowledge, and skill. CPAs are involved with accounting tasks such as producing reports that accurately reflect the business dealings of the companies and individuals for which they work. They are also involved in tax reporting and filing for both individuals and businesses. A CPA can help people and companies choose the best course of action in terms of minimizing taxes and maximizing profitability."[3]

Once I had my CPA help me complete what I thought was a solid business plan I took it back to Ed and life got much easier. My CPA and I met Ed about three times before finally getting his approval. Literally, my last visit with Ed was with my CPA and I sitting in his office, laptops open, working. I remember my CPA saying, "this guy is tough," and getting frustrated because of the many revisions. Finally, we had a product that Ed endorsed, and he got on the phone calling bankers for me.

My hard work paid off. One of the things I am most proud of is that we were about 90% dead on in our projections for the first year even though it

3   https://www.investopedia.com/terms/c/cpa.asp

happened during the 2008 housing market crash. I think it was because we gave ourselves a 10% or 15% cushion just in case we were wrong.

One more thing I did to make sure I had done everything I could to set my business up for success was hire a company to provide a market analysis. A market analysis is a great way to understand the dynamics of the market you are entering. This will help you define your potential customers as well as learn about their purchasing habits and how much they are willing to pay for your services. It will also give you an understanding of your competition, who they are, and what their strengths as well as weaknesses are.

So many people in my life told me I was wasting money. They told me I could do things for a lower cost. They told me I did not need to do all I was doing. I am so glad I didn't listen to them. I have learned over the years that you must pay for quality. Period.

If you half-ass your business plan, expect a half-ass business.

And you can quote me on that! Always, always, always strive to do things right! Take the time you need to. Spend the money you need to. Make the sacrifices you need to. These three things will pay off in the long run.

Move From Struggle to Strength

The Race at Sunrise

Every morning in Africa,
a gazelle wakes up. It knows that it must run
faster than the fastest lion,
or it will be killed.

Every morning a lion wakes up.
It knows that it must outrun the slowest gazelle,
or it will starve to death.

It doesn't matter whether you are a lion

or a gazelle; when the sun comes up,
you had better be running.

—African Parable

I wake up every morning and I run. I always have. This African Proverb was one that I have understood and lived from a very young age. Thinking back on the origin story of Tiki's Playhouse has brought up so many memories for me. As I wrote the beginning of this chapter, I was reminded of how much I struggled through college just to have enough food to eat. Food was scarce! That struggle was real for me.

How does this connect to the subject of this chapter: Stop Talking, Start Doing? I believe the struggles that I went through in these formative years of life have helped me continue to DO rather than TALK. Talking about what I was going to do to put food on the table was never going to put food on the table. Action was the only thing that would see me fed. To be able to pay my own way through school along with all my living expenses, I had to work three jobs. I would survive for months on very little sleep. One summer I remember getting a max of five hours of sleep each day.

I went into the post office from 11pm until 7am to sort mail and shipping. From there I would drive thirty minutes to New Brunswick for my classes, which lasted until 1:30pm. If I didn't have homework or studying to get done, I'd find a quiet place in the library for a nap before heading to the hospital for a 4 until 8pm shift. I'd have a few hours before heading back into the post office.

On the weekends I'd work as a bouncer at a bar on Friday and Saturday nights to make extra money. Those shifts would go from 10pm until about 2 or 3am. From there I'd head into the hospital for a day shift. My boss at the hospital was so supportive. I called her Boss Lady! I know, I know…for some of you readers this might sound derogatory. It really wasn't. I respected her more than so many of my other bosses. She was flexible with my schedule and gave me extra shifts when she could. I also had a key so I could leave my job at the bar and head straight to the hospital for a nap in the Pediatric room before getting up to make coffee for the rest of the team.

To this day Boss Lady and I have remained friends. Rutgers was a difficult time in my life emotionally and financially. I developed great friendships with several co-workers that were very instrumental in helping me "keep my head up." I want to thank Annie, Mary, Karen, Michael, and Renee for helping me stay focused, grounded, and for their loving support! Sure, I could've added my gratitude for these amazing people in the acknowledgements, but I wanted them to read it here.

If you ask any of them, they will tell you: "Kelvin was always coming up with business ideas." I remember wanting to start a delivery service for alcohol. I was going to call it "Liq-a-d-quick". The idea was about fifteen years ahead of its time! The problem was coming up with a system that would accept credit cards. Yes, folks, I could have started my business delivering alcohol and using wireless credit card machines. Does this sound familiar? If only I had focused on the development of the payment system like Square, Instacart, and Drizly did. Hindsight is always 20/20, right?!

Life while in college was grueling. But I was determined to graduate. Receiving a college education and setting myself up for success in life was such a strong motivator that whenever I thought I couldn't do it anymore, when my body was so exhausted and I was mentally broken, I always found a way to push through. This is why people like David Goggins inspire me. Strength, determination, resilience, and dedication are what got me through this time in my life. The lessons I learned have helped me through so many tough times in business as well.

I called this time in my life, when food was so scarce, The Struggle. Why? Because the struggle was real. I found the cheapest food and made it last. I ate a lot of Ramen! Plain noodles with butter and salt was also a common meal in my life at this time. Some days I remember I would open a can of tuna and spread it on a bagel. I would eat half of it in the morning, and if there wasn't any food to be had in a staff meeting at the hospital or pizza to be eaten at the bar later, I would have the other half for dinner.

One of the best memories I have from this time though was the weekly dinners my friends and I would share on Sunday. Food was just as scarce for them as it was for me, but we all still found ways to support each other. Even though the food was not fancy, we enjoyed these dinners. We laughed. We vented. We shared a bond through common experiences. These moments helped us all get through.

In my life now, I have turned this struggle into my strength. In a way it was a gift. It gave me the opportunity to prove to myself and the world around me that I could do it. When I put my mind towards succeeding, I will. I did it then and I do it now!

Shift Your Mindset

It can be hard to take difficult and sometimes heartbreaking or even tragic life events and see them as giving your life some value in a way. Do I wish I had help through college? Do I wish I didn't have to work so hard to achieve my academic goals? Absolutely! But wishing it won't change history. Wishing it is a waste of energy and time. What was, was, and what is, now is. I am stronger for it.

How about you? Is there a time in your life when you struggled? How can you turn that struggle into strength? What skills did that time in your life give you? How can you use them in your business? Take a moment and reflect on these questions. This book is meant to be read with either a journal or an open document by your side. DO THE WORK!

One of the biggest differences between an entrepreneur that succeeds and one that quits is their mindset. What is limiting you? I could've given up in college. It would've been easier to not fight so hard. I could've blamed the world for not giving me an easier ride. I could've let the fact that I didn't have generational wealth to help get an education stop me. I could've let the fact that the world was set up for me to fail stop me. Some days I wanted to. That day in the parking lot, I could've given up. But I didn't.

Why?

Mindset and external motivational factors both played key roles. Let's start with some of the external motivational factors. We all have them. You may have guessed some of mine already, but here they are:

1. To prove everyone who didn't believe in me wrong! The teachers, the friends, the family, the jealous bosses…whoever! THEY WERE WRONG!

2. Systemic racism, both hidden and in plain sight. To the trucks that rev up faster when I cross the road, to the people who walk into my business and walk out after seeing me, to the people who yell racial slurs out their car windows…I am black. I am an entrepreneur. I am a success. And I am not going away. I will never back down!

3. To share my knowledge so that you don't have to make the same mistakes I did. This one is so important to me. I have learned a lot in the last fifteen years. If I can teach you how to avoid having to learn those same lessons the hard way, I am going to do that.

It's good to recognize some of your external motivational factors as you strengthen your mindset. They will help you on the days when your mindset says you can't keep going. Let's move on now to look at your mindset.

I begin this by asking you: What is your internal motivator? What makes you want to be an entrepreneur? In a way here, I am asking you what your WHY is. If your gut response to this question is to answer "money," I am going to challenge you to go deeper. Yes, of course you want to make money. You're starting a business, not applying for a volunteer position. But money is simply a vehicle. It gives you the opportunity to do more, but what you do is what is actually motivated by your why.

For me, the best thing about being in business is that I get to help both people and dogs. When I see a happy dog running and playing, it gives me joy. When I can give their human peace of mind while they are at work, I know I've done a good thing. When someone can come into my coffee shop and feel like they are a part of a welcoming community, this makes the world a brighter place to live. When I get to help someone achieve a fitness goal at my gym, that makes me feel good. During the pandemic I had one client who was struggling with his mental health being isolated and not able to work out. So I gave him the keys to the gym and let him go in on his own. This is my why. I use my work to help others!

Begin your mindset work by writing about what gets you excited. What gets you up in the morning? Why do you do what you do? Your why will be uniquely yours. Maybe you want to do something no one in the world has ever done before. Maybe you have invented something big or small that will make life easier in some way, and your why is to make sure everyone in the world knows about it. This is something that will help you as well on the tough days. So be honest with yourself. Understand your needs and your goals.

Next up in the mindset department is to understand what you currently believe about yourself. How do you talk to yourself? Especially when you fail. Working on strengthening the internal beliefs that lift you up rather than the limiting ones that will knock you down is a lifelong practice. There will be days that knock you down so hard, you will have to work to pull yourself back up. Strengthen the belief that you can succeed at anything you put your mind to, and you will! Why? Because when you believe you can do it, you will take actions that support this belief.

Exercise 2.1
Affirmation Break

Some people love affirmations and some don't. Take this break or leave it. One of the great things about our brains is that we have the ability to change them. The more we think something, the stronger that thought pattern gets.

One of the reasons I think some people don't find affirmations helpful is because it isn't in their own words. A belief about yourself should come from you. Take a moment to create your own success affirmation.

Here are some questions to get you started:

1. What is your strength?

2. How will this strength lead to your success?

3. How can you lean into this strength?

4. What is your success affirmation based on these answers?

Here is a sample answer:

1. My strength is in my resilience.

2. I think that no matter what the universe throws my way, I will get back up and keep going.

3. I lean on this resilience on the days when the punches keep on coming.

4. My affirmation:

   I am strong. I am resilient. I succeed in the face of challenges.

One very important aspect of your mindset is understanding how you feel about failure. You cannot let your fear of failure stop you from taking action. That is the bottom line. Take some time with this and answer the following questions:

1. When have I failed in my life?

2. How did I respond to that failure?

3. What did I learn from that failure?

4. Am I afraid of failure?

5. How can I help myself learn from a failure and move forward?

6. Why is failure a necessary aspect to success?

I am going to talk more about some of the failures I've experienced while on this journey and how I found the strength to keep going in chapter five. For now, I invite you to start getting really honest with yourself about the mindset work you need to do to get comfortable with failing!

Create a Successful Business Plan

Do the work! To end this chapter, I want to bring us back to where I started and recap some of the practical things you need to write a successful business plan. This will prepare you for a deeper dive into understanding the finances of your business in the next chapter.

It comes down to these three things:

One
IF YOU'RE NOT A NUMBERS PERSON, HIRE A NUMBERS PERSON.

You might be too young to have seen the movie this comes from, but I'm sure you've at least heard the saying: "If you build it, they will come." As whimsical and dream-inducing as this sounds, you have to do a lot more than build.

I know a lot of creative people like me who do not want to deal with numbers. But the cold, hard reality is your business will not survive if you do not understand the numbers. You need to get real with yourself here about how much you can actually make and how much it will cost you to make it.

Also, when you are presenting your numbers to potential investors, they will know if you do not understand the financial side of your business. This is not a "fake it until you make it" situation. Hire a CPA or a CA to help you.

Work with a small CPA company, one with maybe one to two employees. Their overhead might not be as high, and this could save you money. Don't be afraid to interview your CPA. They are seeking to come aboard your team, so drill them. You are hiring them. Make sure they are a fit.

Prove to the bank and yourself that you have the knowledge to manage your money!

Two
GET A MENTOR

Seriously! I cannot stress the importance of this enough. Ed at SCORE made me want to quit, but he did right by me. He was tough. He made me angry. But he made me get it right. He gave me some of the tools that ensured my success.

Get yourself a business mentor like Ed! Another great thing about SCORE is that many of the mentors have connections with bankers. If they do, they might be able to set you up to meet with them so that you can begin to understand the bank's process. Start building your network early. If your banker trusts your SCORE representative, things will go a lot smoother when it comes to getting a loan.

Three
HIRE A LOCAL MARKET ANALYSIS COMPANY

Find a local company for your market analysis. This is very important. Chances are your banker will know the market, and if you get someone out of state, good luck getting a loan. Stay local. This will cost you $$$, but it becomes a part of your business plan. The company should package everything up nicely for you so that all you need to do is print it out and attach it to your business plan.

Are you ready to start doing?

Really, I am asking…are you ready? If your answer is *yes*, do not turn the page until you have found the resources you need to write the best business plan for you. Yep, put this book down and start researching your CPA, contact the SCORE chapter (or equivalent) near you, and start looking for a reputable market analyst. Trust me! You will thank me later.

This is your call to stop talking and start doing! When you're ready, I'll see you in the next chapter.

Quick Recap

Work with a mentor for SCORE or a similar organization.

1. Hire a CPA.

2. Pay the big bucks for a reputable local market analysis company.

3. Understand your mindset. Know what your internal and external motivators are.

Chapter 3
Finances, Finances, Finances
How To Work With Banks

The Butterfly of Freedom

"Why do you fly outside the box?"

"I fly outside the box because I can."

"But we know the box. We are SAFE inside the box."

"That, my friend, is why I leave it. For YOU may be safe…

…but I AM FREE."

– Edward Monkton[4]

To start this chapter, I want to share a few memories that bring me so much joy. Being an entrepreneur is tough, but it's worth it. Why? For the freedom to live the way you want to. For those moments that you would never get to experience otherwise.

One of the things my staff and I love to do with our pups, especially on the really hot days, is play with water guns. You should see the looks on the dogs' faces when we first shoot water in their direction. Yes, if you do not know this, dogs are very expressive! It is hilarious. When they realize what is happening, some of them really get into it. Jumping and running in circles and chasing the water. They are so excited. It makes me laugh every time. There is so much joy in their play.

---

4   www.edwardmonkton.com

I have to share another quick, funny memory before we get to the more serious business. I thought of this as I was beginning to brainstorm on some of the unexpected costs you might expect. I'm not even really sure why, but it made me laugh, so here it is:

We were playing with the dogs in one of the rooms when one of the smaller dogs got out. When I found him, he had taken over my dog's bed in my office and was chewing on one of his toys. The funny part was that my rather large dog was staring at this super tiny dog completely perplexed.

He looked up at me as if to say, "Who the heck is this in my bed? What do I do now? Help!"

Dogs! They really do make life so much more fun. Now, onto the business part of this chapter.

The one thing I want you to remember as you continue reading is that dealing with the financial side of your business does get better. I promise. I am not going to tell you that it won't be a struggle at first, but once you make it past your first three years you will start to feel more comfortable. You will feel even better after your first five years. Of course, you will still worry about money, but let me ask you this: Who doesn't?

Think about everyone you know, from someone who has more money than you think you would know what to do with to the family that struggles to put food on the table: everyone worries about money. But you will manage, and with experience you will learn how to save during the highs and ride through the lows.

I am going to share with you some of the toughest lessons I learned when it came to the financial side of my business. I made some mistakes, and my hope in sharing them is that you won't make the same ones. It is one of my biggest motivators in writing this book. If I help just one new business owner not do what I did, then I will have succeeded.

I will have helped at least one person achieve the freedom they desire. Being a successful entrepreneur means freedom for me, and I am willing to give up all the safety and comfort in the world for it! Are you?

My Money Story

Everyone has a money story that begins the moment they are born. You have one. The lady at the grocery store in front of you taking an extra five minutes to get the exact change from the bottom of her purse has one. Your parents have one. I have one.

As you know, I grew up poor. When my brothers and I were young, we were shipped down south to stay with our relatives every summer. It helped ease the financial burden on our parents with us out of the house. But man, my uncles were tough on us. They believed, as my parents did, that idle minds and hands were dangerous. We were destructive boys after all. So they put us to work. I remember thinking, "where's the money? I'm doing all this work for nothing!"

Working for money was something I learned to do very early in my life. I learned that it was a way to buy the things I wanted. As kids, we would go around the neighborhood and offer our services shoveling snow, raking leaves, and cutting grass. It was either make our own money or be forced to wear what our parents bought us. And we did not want to wear what our parents bought us!

There was a time when the supermarket carried sneakers that sat in a basket at the corner of an aisle. I don't recall the name of the brand, but they had four blue stripes. My brothers and I called them Bo-Bo's. We even made up a song:

"Bo-Bo's, they make your feet feel fine.
Bo-Bo's, they cost $1.99.
Bo-Bo's..."

I don't remember the rest of the lyrics, but what I do remember is how much we hated those sneakers. My brothers and I were popular in school because we were great at sports, and the cool kids did not wear Bo-Bo's. Our friends would laugh and call them Adidas knockoffs. So when we did have to wear them, we did our best to rip one of the stripes off and hide our feet as much as possible. Hence the reason why we worked to buy our own clothes.

Another reason why my brothers and I worked to make money was to avoid the embarrassment of getting that white plastic card, the one that allowed us to receive free lunch at school. That card was given to poor kids who couldn't afford to buy lunch. When we did need to use the white card, my brother and I would try to sneak up to the person holding our meal ticket as quickly as possible so we weren't seen. After all, we were known for throwing the best parties at our house, there was our reputation to uphold!

Having our own money to buy lunch allowed us to not only walk right past the ticket person but also to buy what we wanted to eat. The free lunches were limited, and it felt nice to have the freedom to eat whatever we wanted on the menu.

Watching my father struggle the way he did made me not want to do the same. Maybe this is why I started my adult life with a stable career and stuck it out for eight years. What my family's financial struggles also did was instill a strong desire in me to get things right. Even with this desire, however, I still got some things wrong when I was initially financing Tiki's Playhouse. The one thing I did not do was let these setbacks take me down. I kept going. I kept fighting, because in the end the freedom was worth it. Three businesses later, and I feel much more confident, let me tell you!

Dancing with the Devil

If you don't want to dance with the devil, I hope you have enough savings to fund your business yourself! Sure, this devil might be friendly at times. This devil might make you think they have your best interest at heart. Never forget, they are the devil!

Hold your head high and take the lead, but don't get lost in the magic of the moment. Go in knowing exactly what you need and find the bank that will provide that for you.

One of the biggest mistakes I made was choosing the bank that I did. I got lost in the magic of the dance! As you know, my business mentor Ed, from SCORE, had a connection with a banker. Once he was satisfied with my business plan, he set up a meeting with her. She worked at a smaller bank. She was kind and helpful. She was also a minority. It made me feel good to support her by giving her my business, and it excited me as well when she made me an offer.

Let me mention this: In order to dance with the devil, I was supposed to have come to the table with twenty percent of the investment to qualify for an SBA Loan. Simply put, an SBA loan is a small business loan that is partially guaranteed by the government, taking some of the pressure off the bank. The acronym stands for Small Business Administration.

To come up with the initial money, I made some sacrifices. I sold my VW Touareg, which was two years old at the time. I also sold the Rolex I bought myself to celebrate my college graduation, which I was still paying off on my credit card. I know, I know…buying the watch was not the most financially responsible move at the time, but I was so proud of myself for graduating, I needed a reward. That watch meant a lot to me, and yet I was still ready to let it go.

Then I cashed in my 401K and IRA accounts. I also had to pay down debt before I could come to the table for an SBA loan. It was like I was at a roulette table stripping myself of all my possessions on one hand. Always bet on black! Fifteen years later, I guess it was a good hand.

That said, with everything, I was still only able to pull together ten percent of the amount I needed to start. Also, most SBA loans require that you have at least two years of experience running your own business, which I did not.

"Kelvin, why should the bank trust you when you have no experience running your own business and you only have ten percent of the required twenty percent to start?"

"I am used to sacrificing. I have been doing it my entire life. I worked three to four part-time jobs to pay my own way through college. There were times when I ate noodles with butter and pepper for days on end. I will do what I need to survive. I have cashed in my 401K. I've sold things that meant a lot to me."

I bared my heart in my response to her. I continued on to tell her about my dog Tiki and how losing him was devastating. His death was my wake-up call. It was like he was an angel sent in a cute, furry, playful body to remind me I was meant to do this. Tiki's Playhouse would be a reality. I knew it. No matter what I went through, I was determined for it to succeed. It meant more to me than anything.

You know, when I finished talking, we both had tears in our eyes. I was honest. I was truthful. I was passionate. I knew Tiki's would succeed. I just needed the bank to believe in me too. It turns out she would, and her offer would be so much more than I expected it to be in many ways. Some good. Some not so good.

That day I walked out of the bank with $150K more than I asked for. I think I floated out of that office. I closed the deal with the first banker I met. My Uncle Willie always says, "you make your own good luck."

That day, after a year and a half of hard work, I felt like I had made my own good luck.

I had a second meeting with the banker and came out with an additional $250K. In total I received two bank loans totaling $500K. I was so happy. But this is where the story goes south. I was told—that's right, TOLD— where I had to spend the money if I wanted it. At the time I was naïve, green, and happy with the notion of being a business owner. I would do anything they told me to, but somewhere a tiny voice in the back of my mind was saying, "Hey Kelvin, this isn't right. Keep looking. This moment will come back to haunt you later."

Did I listen to that tiny voice of reason in the back of my mind?

No, of course not!

What I didn't realize at the time was that the devil had me. I saw the money and not the cost. That was my first mistake! Don't get it twisted, I liked my banker and still appreciate everything she did to help me get the loan. What I didn't like was the bullshit that comes from taking the devil's money.

In order to get the money, I had to use the vendors that already had a relationship with the bank. For example, I had to switch from the CPA I had used to develop my business plan to the one the bank gave me. I also had to work with the marketer they suggested and agree to spend over $100K on marketing in the first year. THE FIRST YEAR! I had radio ads and billboards and newspaper ads. Let me tell you, I have spent years paying off that marketing bill. Looking back, I know I never would have ever signed on for that had I not been forced to.

That lesson was a huge one. The debt at times felt crippling and much of it, like the marketing, was unnecessary. They also made me use their designer to help me create the look of the daycare. This also was a cost that I could've avoided, as I already had a clear idea of what a good doggy daycare—one that encouraged happy, playful pups to enjoy their time—looked like.

In hindsight I should have walked into that first meeting at the bank with both my business lawyer and CPA. But instead, I had my blue suit and black wingtip shoes to keep me grounded in reality! Ha! The whole time I thought I was hot shit. Okay, the suit and the shoes were really nice, but in the end they cost me thousands of dollars over the years. That suit should have been made of gold!

My advice would be to do your homework. Go to your meetings with the bank ready to negotiate. Remember that no matter how excited, prepared, or arrogant you are, you will never ever be fully prepared to deal with the devil. The devil is smooth. The devil is smart. And most importantly, if you are not prepared, the devil will always win. The system is designed that way.

Get a team of people to help you. Bring a CPA. Bring a lawyer. Yes, it will cost you money, but I have learned the hard way that you have to pay for success. Remember this point anytime you find yourself wanting to cut corners:

You have to pay for success.

Align yourself with professionals, not family members, friends, your buddy, or frat brother. Get people in your corner that will tell you the truth. Remember Mike Tyson. He lost his title fight to Buster Douglas because his corner was not prepared. In his corner he had *yes* men. Mike lost the fight even before he entered the ring.

Hire professionals who will tell you the truth, not simply try to please you. They should push you to see when you are making terrible mistakes, even if you don't want to hear them. That is integrity. Make sure you hire people who love what they do and care about you as a client, meaning they are willing to get fired if you don't like what you hear.

Pay the price for success.

Get a financial person you can trust. Rather than a larger firm, hire a small business owner to do your bookkeeping and CPA work. Why? Because their reputation is on the line. They are just like you. They live on referrals. They also work day and night trying to build their business. This is not to say that big firms and companies can't do the work. I am sure they can. My experience has been that small business owners do it better. Small business owners do it right. You are not a number, and the CPA you work with is not simply a cog in a very big machine.

Surround yourself with professionals, not family or friends. Pay for it. Trust it. Believe in it.

Finally, don't just meet with one bank. Meet with several. Try out the big ones and the small ones. The devil will do its best to intimidate you. Don't let it. Always remember that you are their client. When you borrow money from them, they make money. Without you and others like you, they would not have a business. Find the right bank for you and your needs. If they are forcing you to pay for thousands of dollars' worth of marketing that you do not feel you need, listen to your gut. Listen to that voice in the back of your head saying, "hey…heeeeyyyy, remember me. This isn't right. Let's go somewhere else. Let's keep looking."

When Dealing with the Devil

Go prepared! To help you get started I am going to share a list of questions to ask each banker you meet. I say each, because I want to highlight just how important it is to meet with many of them. Not just one or two, but as many as it takes to find the one that is right for you and your business. Also remember to bring a CPA and lawyer with you to each meeting. Lean on the professionals!

Questions to bring to your bank meetings: .

1. Who determines the loan approval?

2. How many people are involved in the approval process?

    The more people, the more questions and information to provide. Attempt to find out if the underwriter/s are available to discuss your loan. More than likely the answer is no, but why not ask?

3. What are the terms of the loan?

    If they are asking you to spend $100K on marketing you don't believe you need, walk away! I repeat: WALK AWAY! Run fast and don't look back!

4. Can I refinance in a few years? If so, what will the requirements be for refinancing?

    Refinancing is important, especially if you have a higher interest than desired.

5. If I decide to pay the loan off early, is there an early termination fee?

6. Do I have to offer personal collateral to secure the loan? If so, what are the details?

7. After paying back a determined amount of money, can the collateral be released?

Meaning, if you have paid back fifty percent of your bank loan, can all collateral be released? Try to get your personal collateral back as quickly as possible. The goal is to keep all the finances related to the business connected to the business and not your personal finances.

8. What would it take to apply for another loan if my business is in good standing?

Try and secure the ability to get additional loans in the beginning. Why do this? Just in case something like another pandemic hits, you have the ability to get additional capital if needed. If possible, get it in writing. This is why you need an attorney. The bank will protect themselves. Period. Get as much terminology in your favor before signing the loan documents. Yes, it will cost you in legal fees, and don't forget you need a CPA to review the financial terms of the loan. Spend the money in the beginning and increase your odds.

Tips to Secure Financing

Get your three-year Pro Forma Plan right!

This is a big one. Like I have already said, I got the help I needed and put in the blood, sweat, and so many tears on this one. It was frustrating and it made me want to quit, but it paid off in the end.

In my experience the banker skipped past all the beginning fluff and went straight to the meat of it, my three-year Pro Forma Plan. Focus on the numbers and market analysis instead of bragging about yourself. The banker is reading you in the present moment, not on paper. Be confident. Be transparent. Know your stuff!

They are looking at how you answer questions, how nervous you are, and if you are prepared. Don't worry about creating a colorful presentation, just get to the numbers.

Show Your Commitment

The banker wants to know how committed you are to your plan. Before going to meet with the banks, ask yourself:

What am I willing to sacrifice to make it happen?

If you haven't done this already, sit down and write out all the things you are willing to sacrifice in your life to ensure the financial success of your business. Get really clear about it. Be honest with yourself. It's okay if you do not want to sell a car that you love or if you're not willing to offer up your house as collateral. No judgment. Just answer honestly.

Know that the bank will want to see a commitment to the success of your business. How can you show this commitment to them? If you're having a hard time answering the first question, try answering this one and then going back.

One thing I know for sure is if you want your business to succeed, you have to commit completely. Your first small business is not a side hustle, it's a full-time commitment, with overtime! How will you prepare for this in your life?

Prepare for the Unexpected

The first year of your business is crucial. You will want to have built a healthy cushion into your projections to cover any of the unexpected expenses. You also want to make sure that you have enough money in your own personal savings to not have to pay yourself this first year. You need the time to build the financial strength of your business. This was another one of my big mistakes. I did not have the savings to put all my earnings back into the business.

Yes, this means that if your bills are $2,500 a month, you should have at the very least $30,000 saved for yourself.

My first year in business was not easy. It was also the year President Obama was elected and the housing market crashed.

I remember crying in the rain while walking dogs yelling at GOD: "Why now? Why is this happening? Why does everything have to be so hard? Can't you just give me something here?"

My townhouse went into foreclosure three times. I had to borrow money to keep my home. I didn't get paid for two years straight. NOT A SINGLE CENT. I had to pay my employees first.

It was hard. I was uncomfortable but I did survive.

My landlord reduced my rent for two years to help me get through the recession of 2008/2009. If it was not for him, I would have folded. My landlord has been in my corner since day one and I can't be more appreciative of him. That man has single-handedly kept me in business. He took a big risk on me: A kid with no business experience and no business degree, just a will to survive and a solid business plan. I guess I had the eye of the tiger.

This story actually brings me to a really good point. Be transparent with both the bank and your landlord. They will often be more understanding when you get into trouble. Let them know exactly what is happening and what plans you've put in place to recover from it. I will even provide my P/L (profit and loss statements) and give access to view my bank accounts when necessary. Give them a clear idea of when you will be able to catch up on your payments. Honesty is always the best policy. People can often see right through a lie and will be less willing to help you out when you need it. There are good people out there. Take my landlord as an example!

Let's take a moment to look beyond some of the bigger national or global events (remember the pandemic?!) to some of the smaller things that can take your business down if you do not have a contingency plan, like unexpected tax bills or an overflowing toilet or a fridge on the fritz or a computer crash. I have had three of my computers crash in the past three years. Yes, THREE!

In my business, sometimes it's a cute pup that can accidentally cause a bit of havoc in the day. I was in my office when my dog walked past and pulled the plug on the computer. He kept going about his business and I did not notice right away. I thought I had lost so much information. Customer data, payments...Luckily a friend of mine was able to recover everything in this case, and it taught me a valuable lesson. Ever since, I complete an external backup every single day!

It does not matter how prepared you are, there will be costs that come at you from left field. Prepare for them by padding your projections and having funds available to cover both them and you.

Cash flow, cash flow, cash flow!

One of the best pieces of advice I can give you in all of this is to have money.

"Wait a second, Kelvin, isn't the whole point of this chapter on finance to help me get the money I need because I don't have money?"

Of course, but what I mean is that you should always find ways to make sure the cash is flowing in. If your business is experiencing a low cash flow month, figure out a way to fix it. Here are some of my strategies:

1. Offer a sale. Something like: Buy a pack of ten afternoon play dates for your sweet doggie and receive an extra 20% off the regular discount. Or, bring your scruffy pup in for spa day within the next week and receive 50% off your next visit.

2. Create a new product within the realm of what your business offers, that is something you can do without extra cost, and offer exclusive access to be one of the first to try it.

3. Throw some kind of special event or party that you can sell tickets for, and also highlight your product. Keep this simple though, as throwing

events can be costly and the point is to have the cash flowing in, not out!

4. Get creative and offer new unique services. Think outside the box. Be original with your creativity.

Do your research. Look to the government for any small business grants you can apply for. Your local chamber of commerce or county development center may also have some information. Go to the SCORE website and check out the information they have posted there. Often you will find that there is money available that you had no idea you could access.

Exercise 3.1
Rewrite Your Money Story

There are some people in this world who see money as evil. They equate it with greed, ruthlessness, and violence. The thing is: money is simply a tool. It is neither good nor bad. Having more money simply amplifies who you already are.

It's time to grab your journal again. Put the book down at this point and write about what a day in your life looks like after five years in business. How has your business grown? What does the freedom of owning your own business feel like? What do you do when you wake up in the morning? And what do you do with the rest of your day?

Have fun with this one. Let go. Dream big. You are a success!

Quick Recap

1. Remember that it gets better. You've got this! Keep going.

2. Know that failure happens. Without failure you won't succeed.

3. Learn from your mistakes and move forward.

4. When choosing a CPA, look for a small business rather than a larger one.

5. Your three-year Pro Forma Plan is important! Get it right and you won't regret it.

6. Save enough personally to not have to pay yourself for at least a year.

7. Go to at least three bankers before deciding.

8. Bring a lawyer and CPA with you to meet the banker.

9. Expect the unexpected, and have a cushion to pay for it.

10. Be transparent with your lenders and landlord if you hit hard times.

Chapter 4
Go Hug A Tree!
How To Get Creative

The Handwriting on the Wall

CHANGE HAPPENS
They keep moving the cheese.

ANTICIPATE CHANGE
Get ready for the cheese to move.

MONITOR CHANGE
Smell the cheese often
so you know when it is getting old.

ADAPT TO CHANGE QUICKLY
The quicker you let go of old cheese,
the sooner you can enjoy new cheese.

CHANGE
Move with the cheese.

ENJOY CHANGE!
Savor the adventure
and the taste of new cheese!

BE READY TO QUICKLY
CHANGE AGAIN AND AGAIN
They keep moving the cheese

–Spencer Johnson[5]

Have you ever read the book *Who Moved My Cheese?* If not, I highly recommend it. It is one of my favorites! In this book, Spencer Johnson uses the story of two mice named Sniff and Scurry and two Little people named Hem and Haw in their hunt for cheese to help his readers understand the importance of change in their lives.

His story reminds us that in life and in business, things are in constant motion. The proverbial cheese, be it success or money or simply a feeling of accomplishment, will get moldy over time or be moved by someone else or won't be there for you in the beginning or will be moved again or you might even misplace it. You either give up on the cheese and go starving or embrace the adventure and find some new, delicious cheese!

I begin this chapter on creativity talking about change to make a very specific point:

When you are afraid of change, lean into your creativity.

It is your creativity that will help you find the answer you need.
It is your creativity that will inspire you to get uncomfortable.
It is your creativity that will inspire you to stay uncomfortable until you succeed.
It is your creativity that won't let you stay comfortable for long.

It is also your creativity that brings you the ultimate joy!
A joy that gets you up in the morning, ready and grateful for the day.
A joy that asks you to settle for nothing less than awesome.

In the end, it is your creativity that will see that you always have cheese! In my own life, it is my creativity that drives me. It is also the thing that sets me

---

5   Johnson, S. (1999). *Who moved my cheese?* Vermilion.

apart from the crowd. In this chapter I am going to ask you to dig deep into your own creativity. To do this I am going to use the Spencer Johnson quote I shared with you. If you don't have your computer or your journal beside you, now is the time to get it!

Exercise 4.1
Change Happens!
They keep moving the cheese.

Write about a time in your life when you had something taken from you. In that moment you had to either find it again or move on to something else.

For example, you started a new business. It was going well, but then new competition opened up just around the corner. How did you set yourself apart? How did you use the situation to your benefit?

Create Strong Roots

A friend once told me to hug a tree when I was feeling sad. A tree is deeply rooted and in balance with the earth. Her point was that the tree would remind me that I too am connected to the earth and have strong roots. I have strong roots because I worked at developing them. I have worked hard in all areas of my life. Those roots were created with strength, resilience, love, a desire to do good, and most importantly my creativity.

In times of both sadness as well as joy, I can depend on the strong roots I have created to keep me grounded. Those roots also help me withstand the storms.

Let's take this metaphor and expand on it. Imagine your creativity being like an entire tree growing on the side of a mountain. During most of its life, it faces harsh winds and heavy snowfall and yet it flourishes. It flourishes because of its creative, strong, and resilient roots. They grow deep into the earth creating a strong base from which to grow. It is a part of your strength and your resilience.

Just like that tree, if you are not deeply committed to your creativity there will be no stability in your business. You will not withstand even the first storm you face. Committing to your creativity as an entrepreneur means believing in your dreams, because if you don't believe in your dreams no one else will.

Keep moving forward through the doubt. Creativity has no friends, just possibilities. Creativity does not care what the doubters think, it just asks you to keep creating. Your creativity is built on your life experience and your life experience alone. Your creativity is you!

If I told you how many times people laughed or chuckled under their breaths over ideas that I had, you would be amazed. Or maybe you wouldn't, maybe you have experienced it too. Let them laugh! I have come to a place in my own life where I thrive on the laughter of others. Learn to let their laughter inspire you to create more. Let it inspire you to free your creativity. Don't stop yourself from getting outrageously creative in your thinking.

I once heard Steve Harvey speak about how God helps you find your way in life through the ideas that were keeping you from sleeping at night. This really resonated with me because I completely agree. I think ideas are God's way of providing you with answers. The problem is you won't hear them if you are afraid to listen and challenge yourself. If you don't challenge yourself, you will never be successful.

Sure, you may have a home, experience financial freedom, and be able to provide for your family, but if you do not challenge yourself to keep growing, you have failed. Truly wealthy people challenge themselves to continuously reinvent themselves. They are constantly learning. They are always searching for new opportunities.

This is why I love Shark Tank. Mark Cuban, one of the main Sharks, has over a hundred and ninety companies in his portfolio and twelve people helping him run them. Wow! These companies range from sports to AI to food to biotech to clothing and more. The lesson here: diversify! So far, my business portfolio includes companies that range from dogs to coffee to fitness to whiskey and I am working on more. Take risks. Learn something new. Don't be afraid to walk alone in the dark.

Failure creates success! Let me say that again, FAILURE CREATES SUCCESS! You must be willing to fail over and over and over again before your creativity comes alive! Grow some tough skin when all around you people are throwing darts of jealousy, envy, or resentment because they are too afraid to either get creative or to take action on their creativity. Remember, people who are afraid to fail will work to spread their negativity. Don't be fooled. Oftentimes the people who do this are not bad people, they just feel better about their choices when they are keeping you down with them. Don't let them.

Rise above. Listen to the ideas running through your head. Keep a journal beside your bed at night so you can write them down. Sometimes this helps me to fall asleep.

If it has been a while since you've listened to your creative nudges, start to create space in the day to just think of new ideas or give voice to the ones you have been ignoring. Lean into your creativity every single day and you will be forced to grow. You won't have a choice!

Exercise 4.2
ANTICIPATE CHANGE
Get ready for the cheese to move.

One of the best things you can do as an entrepreneur is set yourself up for success by having some new and creative ideas ready to go for when the cheese moves!

Write about one of your most outrageously creative ideas. One that you have never told anyone for fear that they might think you are crazy. Or maybe it's one you are so excited about that you've shared it and have been laughed at. Or maybe it's one you are developing right now. Get crazy creative!

Understand What A Creative Response to Change Is

How you respond to change is everything! You will either thrive or call it quits. Change comes in many different forms throughout our lives. Sometimes you see it coming and can ride the wave to shore. Sometimes it dropkicks you in the gut and you can do nothing but writhe on the ground for a bit until the pain subsides. Sometimes you are walking along on a beautiful morning and feel a call to walk down a different path.

We all know that the one constant in life is that it will change.

Being a business owner means hugging a tree daily, metaphorically speaking of course. Remind yourself you are strong, feel your connection to the earth and to your purpose. Remind yourself that you are committed and work to get even more creative every single day.

A lot of people confuse the idea of being creative with being an artist or a dancer or a writer. Of course all the arts require creativity, but you don't have to be an artist to be creative. I've met so many people who say, "oh, I'm not creative," when in fact they are.

The actual definition of creativity is very simple, it means *the ability to create*. It doesn't define what you create or how you create. Humans create! You are inherently a creative being. I speak this truth as a reminder that you have the ability to adapt to change quickly, easily, and fearlessly when you lean into your creative side.

Think about it this way:

You have spent all afternoon preparing an amazing meal for your relatives for Thanksgiving. At 5pm a whole bunch of hungry faces will be waiting to taste your creations. It's 3pm now and everything is running smoothly, or so you think. What you don't realize at the time is that you've misjudged how long it will take to cook the turkey. It always annoyed you that your parents served a dry, over-cooked bird and you had always vowed to put a juicy, perfectly cooked bird on the table. Maybe this was your mistake!

It's now 4:30, and everyone has arrived hungry! Feeling stressed as you read this story yet? They are sitting in the living room chatting and laughing when you figure out you've made a mistake. The turkey needs at least another hour. What do you do? Grandma will judge. Your brother-in-law will get hangry. The kids will impatiently start going crazy.

"This is a disaster," you think to yourself. But wait, is it though? Or is it an opportunity?

There are a few ways you could handle the situation:

1. *You could walk out into the living room and face the firing squad.*

2. *You could use this as an opportunity to add a new fun tradition to your family's Thanksgiving.*

You choose the latter!

You quickly make sure all the other dishes are being kept warm and pull the gravy off the stove for the moment. You walk confidently into the other room and announce:

"Today, we are going to play a game!"

There are groans throughout the room. You ignore them. You know Grandma loves singing and she is the one to please!

"We are going to sing for our supper! Grandma will pick the song and be the judge! The winner gets to fill their plate first. Which means…you get your favorite part of the bird."

At first, people are shy. But you jump in and make it a silly, good time. Did they figure you had messed up the turkey? Maybe. Did it matter in the end? Not one bit! Did your new tradition create an incredible memory for your family? Absolutely!

There are three lessons to be learned from this story that apply directly to the way you think about business:

1. You limit your creativity by letting the judgment of others get in the way. Going back to my earlier point, let them laugh and do it anyway.

2. You can adapt quickly to change by getting creative.

3. When you listen to your creative nudges, you have the ability to create great things. You may even be able to change lives!

A real-life example of a time when I had to use my own creativity to make an unexpected change better was during the three-month state of emergency caused by Covid-19. Although I was allowed to stay open during this time to accommodate the doggy daycare needs for essential workers, I recognized that the community needed more. I opened up my doggie playground for dogs to come and play for free on Saturday mornings. It gave people a reason to get out of their homes and a place for the dogs to stay social, happy, and playful.

It also brought people to my coffee shop on those mornings, adding some extra weekend revenue. After the emergency order was lifted, I began to charge a five-dollar entry fee to cover some of the fees to run the program as not everyone who came would purchase a beverage or treat. I adapt to the changes as they flow my way. It is the only way!

Exercise 4.3
ADAPT TO CHANGE QUICKLY
The quicker you let go of old cheese,
the sooner you can enjoy new cheese.

Use the botched turkey dinner example to help you with this exercise. Remember that when life throws you a challenge and you need to shift gears, you always have a choice: you can admit defeat or make the moment even better than it would have been.

Write about something in your life that you always do. In many ways you accept it as it is, but you don't enjoy it anymore or you are simply going through the motions because you know it needs to be done. It could be a family tradition, or a task at home, or something to do with your business. From here, think outside the box. If you were forced at a moment's notice to adapt to change, how could you get creative to make it better?

Let Joy Guide You

About seven years ago, my brain was wandering, as it is apt to do when it should be sleeping. It was almost Christmas and I began to think about the dogs that were already booked to stay at Tiki's. Often, people have to travel out of town, and they either don't want to put their dog through the stress of travel or it's just not possible to bring them.

As you know, I love my dogs. I began to think about how I could make the holidays special for them too, especially since they couldn't be with their families. When you think about Thanksgiving or Christmas or weddings or any time you get together with your family to celebrate, what comes to mind? FOOD!

Every year during the Thanksgiving and Christmas holidays, I cook for the dogs on my Big Green Egg. This brings me so much joy. I love making the food and preparing the plates. The great thing about dogs is that they have no idea if you messed up the turkey and need another half hour!

We always send pictures to the parents around dinner time so that they can "have dinner" with their dogs. They absolutely love it. Everyone is missing their furry family member, and it brings them joy to share in a special moment with them while they are away.

The best part of these dinners is watching the dogs pig out on the food. It's so funny to see them attack the meat, which is usually turkey or chicken, while leaving the veggies and rice. Over the years we have refined the process. Once all the food is prepared, we plate it for the photos and then we throw it all in a big bowl and chop it up before we portion it out for the pups. I don't think I can describe in words just how much fun this is for me and how much joy it brings.

When I thought of this event, I was not thinking about how it could make money or bring me more customers. It was just my creativity being driven by my desire to bring more joy. But it is now one of the things that makes Tiki's Playhouse even more special than it was before. It is unique to me.

This is an example of a small change I made to my business by choice, which asked me to do a bit more work but ultimately paid me millions in joy currency!

Take a Creative Leap

There are two types of creativity in the world. First there is the safe kind. Remember, the definition of creativity is to create something. It can be anything. It doesn't judge. You can make a delicious loaf of bread. You adapted it from an old family recipe and have made it a hundred times before. You can paint a million paintings based on one theme. Many artists do this. You know this theme. You do it well. You create beautiful paintings without worrying that they will miss the mark.

There is nothing wrong with safe creativity, at least until it comes to your success as an entrepreneur. This is my belief anyway. I think that to become the best version of your entrepreneurial self you need to regularly employ the second type of creativity, which is the "holy shit I'm terrified I'll fail but I'm going to do it anyway" creativity. It's all about risk, and without it the reward will always fall short.

I know I have been in business for as long as I have because I take a lot of creative risks. Not only that, but I am open and ready to listen. I adapt to creativity by accepting what comes to me in the middle of the night as a gift from GOD. Creativity is about exploring change.

Think about why you enjoy your creativity. What about either the process or the end product makes you sing? And then dive into that, just like I did with the holiday dinners for my pups. I enjoy the whole process of that creative journey.

Another thing my creativity gives me is the joy of seeing my logo on products. I love that! It gives me so much pride in that moment when I look at something and can say, "I made that thing!" I really appreciate how people respond to my creativity. It truly gives me joy. So much joy that I am always ready to jump into another project, concept, idea, or business venture.

"Keep the creativity coming in the middle of the night. I'll sleep when I'm dead!" I say.

I love getting new ideas while driving down the street listening to music, or while watching tv and seeing something that sparks my creative brain. Or while having a "board meeting" (I'll tell you more about these later). Taking the time to decompress and listen to silence is often when the next big project comes to me. I guess this is why I am more like my father. My dad always thought outside the box and never gave up on his dreams. My dad is over seventy years old and still hitting the pavement everyday talking about the next biggest thing! This will be me until my final day on this earth. I will always allow my creativity to drive me.

Exercise 4.4
ENJOY CHANGE!
Savor the adventure
and the taste of new cheese!

Take yourself on an adventure with this exercise. Think about one big change you want to make in your life right now. Ask yourself:

1. Why do I want to make this change?

2. What scares me about making this change?

3. How will making this change improve my life?

An Inspirational Success Story

Success is not always about money. It is about so much more. After so many years I am proud to be able to provide opportunities for my employees. SUCCESS! I have paid all my bank loans back without any issues. SUCCESS!

I grew up with my dad bouncing checks left and right. I am proud to say that through all the tough times, I have never bounced a check as a business owner and my employees have always been paid on time. There have been many times that I paid late fees to the IRS because I had to pay my employees before the government. SUCCESS! I have never missed a bank loan payment or car note. SUCCESS!

I continue to live my purpose, even when the challenges threaten to break me. SUCCESS! I share my experiences with others so they can learn from them in the ways I have. SUCCESS! I continue to learn and grow. SUCCESS! I inspire others to live in their purpose. SUCCESS!

That said, I know I have not yet reached the success level that awaits me. God has a plan for me, and I will continue to be resilient and anticipate creativity. I will take advantage of every new thought, concept, and idea that pops into my head. It's in my DNA.

Sometimes when I am having an off day, I wonder what it would be like to return to a nine to five job. A guaranteed vacation. Weekends off. Not having to write paychecks. Being stress free. How would my life be different right now if I did? Would I be writing this book? Would I want to pay it forward? I don't know. What I do know is I am living my best life NOW! I love the stress, challenges, disappointment, frustrations, and pain that come with being an entrepreneur. Why? Michael Jordan. Kobe Bryant. Shaq. Tiger Woods. Serena Williams…

Being an entrepreneur is all about stepping out of your comfort zone. No safety nets! You are the safety net. If you are not willing to be your own safety net, Amazon is hiring. Ouch! Did reading that last line make you angry? Did it light a fire in you to do everything you can to live with intention in your purpose no matter what lessons you have to learn? I hope so!

Take a moment now to think about what success means to you. Dig deep and think hard about it. Simply saying that you want to be rich isn't enough to drive you up the mountain through a blizzard.

YOU are my reason today! YOU are here and I can't wait to read your success story one day too! To end this chapter, I want to share with you a success story that inspires me in life and also in the boardroom! Have you ever heard of Uncle's Nearest Whiskey? If not, I highly recommend it. Not only because the story of the man who made it is incredibly inspiring, but also because it is a really good whiskey. The man knew what he was doing and did it well!

Nathan (Nearest) Green, a formerly enslaved man from just outside Lynchburg is known as the Godfather of Tennessee Whiskey. Once a free man he continued to work on the Dan Call Farm, where he was able to perfect his craft and support his family. He took the opportunity that presented itself to him, through Reverend Call's love of whiskey and the use of the still that he had on his farm, and created something great! In all of it, I am sure Nearest faced trials and tribulations, but he pushed forward. Being a newly freed man didn't mean life was easy for him.

According to Fawn Weaver, CEO of Uncle Nearest Whisky, Nearest taught Jack Daniel how to make his legendary whiskey. Now a household name throughout North America, it makes me smile whenever I see a bottle of Jack Daniel's. "Way to go, Nearest! You are a legend!"

The best part of this story is that his own legacy is now becoming more widely known. To date, Uncle Nearest is in fifty states and twelve countries. The main thing I want you to take away from this story is that talent and creativity do not come easily, and neither do opportunities. It takes effort and perseverance. You cannot simply wish for success and hope it will magically appear. Let your hard work speak for itself!

Exercise 4.5
BE READY TO QUICKLY
CHANGE AGAIN AND AGAIN
They keep moving the cheese

Write about what success means to you right now, at this moment. Come back to this writing again and again and again, and rewrite what success means to you throughout your life.

Quick Recap

1. Know that change is inevitable.

2. Embrace change.

3. Anticipate change and prepare for it.

4. Shift your mindset to enjoy change rather than fear it.

5. Think on your feet and adapt to change quickly.

6. Lean into your creativity. It is your most useful tool when dealing with change as an entrepreneur.

Chapter 5
Expect the Unexpected
How To Navigate The Things You Can't Plan For

Have you ever heard the phrase "God only gives us what we can handle"? I completely disagree! I think God, or the universe or whatever you want to call it, gives you more than you can handle. You are not here to be comfortable. You are here to learn and to grow and to make this world a better place. This is what I believe and this is how I live.

Each day I strive to be better, no matter what challenges I encounter. God has a higher purpose for me, and this is why I keep going. If I had stayed in my stable, secure office job I would not have the opportunity to live my purpose. I know that I am meant to lead. This is what drives me.

Again, I lean into my why, my purpose, my reason for being here. I believe it is to use my own creativity to create opportunities for others. What does this mean? It means that I get to use my experiences to help others achieve their goals, especially in becoming an entrepreneur. If you have the desire to walk the path, I want to be able to help. I think anyone who has a dream and a true desire to start a business of their own should have the opportunity to do it.

No matter how difficult my plight may have been, I offer the exact same experience as the entrepreneurs on Shark Tank. I may not be able to offer money or partnership right now, but I feel the knowledge I have to share will take your business from an unknown to securing you a place to pitch on Shark Tank. This book is the start of that mission for me. If I can help passionate entrepreneurs set themselves up for greater success in their first—or even second or third—business, it will be a win! This is my big blue sky dream!

Exercise 5.1
Blue Sky Moment

Before we dive into some of the unexpected things I have encountered in both my personal and professional life, I want to get you into dreamer mode. Because above all else, you are a creator! That is why you're here. Your creativity has the ability to get you through. Lean into it!

Give yourself some time to complete this exercise. Get your journal and find a relaxing place where you won't be disturbed. Maybe there is a nearby park or a beautiful spot in your backyard.

Look up at the big blue sky and dream. Dream big. Don't let that voice in your head saying you can't do it get in the way. Then write your big dream down…all of it!

To get you inspired I want to share more of mine with you. A part of my big blue sky dream is to have multiple successful business chains. I'd love to see Tiki's Playhouse expand across the country so that all dogs have an opportunity to play and stay in environments that allow them to thrive. Once I have these businesses successfully running, I want to be able to support other entrepreneurs by funding their business. Think Shark Tank, but Kelvin style!

This example is short and I haven't gone into much detail, mostly because this exercise is for you! Get into it. Dive really deep. Put in all the details. What does it feel like to have a successful business? What do your days look like? What is your impact on your own life, the lives of your loved ones, your community, and the world. Like I said, think big. The sky is limitless!

Life Lessons Learned Early

Music has the ability to lift you up. It brings you out of yourself, out of your dark thoughts, and connects you back with the world around you. You are not alone. The challenges you face will be unique to your life, but there are others out there who have experienced a similar kind of pain or situation.

Whenever I can, I use music to lift me up and inspire me to keep fighting! Some songs give me the space to release my emotions and some songs give me my battle cry!

I have some tough stories I want to share with you in this chapter. One thing I hope you are coming to understand about me as you read this book is that I always aim to be truthful and transparent. You do not have to have everything figured out to be an authority on what you do. You do not have to have a fancy car or earn seven figures before you start giving back to the world.

Some nights I don't sleep because my brain is either dreaming or worrying! I have faced some major health issues that have demanded I get even more resilient in the face of those challenges. My journey will be my journey and yours will be uniquely yours. I share some of the unexpected things that have happened to me to not only help you prepare, but also to help you see that you are not alone when the unexpected happens to you.

Many of the events I have gone through and continue to go through are things that helped me grow. Do I wish some of them didn't happen? Of course I do! But I do think the tough stuff happens for a reason. It is meant to test you. It is meant to push you to your limits. It is meant to give you the tools you need to succeed, to face the challenges with courage and strength.

As you know, I faced many challenges throughout my childhood, but one of the most unexpected ones happened just before my twin brother and I were about to graduate high school. Imagine being woken up in the middle of the night by people who were taking your home.

Suddenly we were forced out onto the street with as many belongings as we could push to a friend's house. Our dog was let out by the Sheriff's department and ran away. Eventually my dad found him and kept him at his office.

At the time, my dad was not home. It was just me, my mom, and my twin brother. I can't explain how traumatic this experience was.

The foreclosure caused my parents to split. Once the dust settled, my twin and I decided to go live with my dad. Their relationship had been souring for years and some of it had to do with my dad neglecting his duties with our family and at home. But shortly after they split, we would find out there was more to the story.

My dad bought a townhouse in a nicer area of town, but more importantly for me and my brother, he worked all the time. We could go back to being the fun party house we once were. For one hot minute, things were okay.

What comes next is something that changed me and life forever. I was completely blindsided when my dad came home one day and said, "It's her or you!"

On that fateful day, my dad asked to speak with me and my brother just before we were about to leave for our commute to college. He gave us a very clear ultimatum: accept his new fiancée or get out of his house. We had been bamboozled a week or so before with the announcement of his engagement to his female business partner. We hated this woman with every fiber of our young bodies. We knew she wasn't right for our father or for our family. It hurt me so much that my dad would choose her over me. There are two people in the world that you should be able to trust to keep you safe: your mom and your dad. My dad broke my trust forever that day.

My brother and I decided to leave that weekend. My mother had a one-bedroom apartment. We could sleep there temporarily but could not live with her permanently. We both adapted to our new and very unexpected reality. From having a home to live in to having to not only cover the financial cost of school but also our living expenses was a tough blow. As you know, we worked multiple jobs to financially support ourselves through college.

So, there was another lesson my father taught me about being an entrepreneur:

Expect the unexpected and adapt quickly or fail miserably.

I cut my dad out of my life for ten years. That experience left scars that I am still dealing with today. Emotionally, I know that my work will be ongoing. Like I said, losing trust in the one person who is meant to protect you can be devastating. My brother and I still talk about the things we were hurt by to this day.

There was a point in my life when I knew I needed to make peace with my dad, not only for him but for me. It wasn't until we all thought he was going to die that I called him. He was living in Malaysia at the time and had contracted malaria. It was at that moment that I was able to remember the good in him. While he ultimately chose a woman to whom he would only be married for two years over us, he had really strived hard to raise us right. He succeeded. All three of his boys are college educated and law abiding citizens. We are successful in our own ways, but not only that, we are good people. My dad was a part of that. And so, in many ways, even though he caused us much pain, I am grateful for all he did for me.

Unexpected Health Issues

There is a fantastic song called "Never Would Have Made It" by an incredible artist, Marvin Sapp. It is all about becoming stronger and wiser because of the storm. Let me tell you, this song helped me through some of my toughest days and my darkest nights. When I was yelling, "Why God? Why is this happening?" to the heavens, it was these lyrics that reminded me to keep fighting. To keep going. Some of the ongoing health issues I have faced require a lot of strength!

One of the first unexpected things to jump in my path in my business was something that I never thought could happen. You hear about these things and the doctors warn you, but it was devastating. I had already put the plans in motion to start Tiki's Playhouse. I was still working on my business plan when I had to have hip surgery. No, this isn't the worst part!

The worst part is that I developed MRSA. What is MRSA, you ask?

MRSA is "any of several strains of a bacterium (*Staphylococcus aureus*) that are resistant to methicillin and related antibiotics (such as penicillin) and typically live harmlessly on skin and mucous membranes but may cause usually mild infections of the skin or sometimes more severe infections (as of the blood, lungs, or bones) especially in hospitalized or immunocompromised individuals."[6]

The likelihood of getting an MRSA infection in a surgical site is between one and three percent.[7] Yes, I had a ninety-seven percent chance of not getting MRSA and experiencing a smooth recovery! Ninety-seven percent! Unfortunately, my reality was one of the worst-case scenarios. What that meant for me was the need to remove the hip they put in and replace it again, but not until I had recovered from the infection. Because MRSA is so contagious, I had to be isolated in the hospital behind double glass doors. Anyone who came to visit had to wear a mask.

The chaplain was called down to speak with me because I was not eating. I was so sad about the situation. Basically, I was bedridden for two weeks with my right hip removed to clean out the infection in my hip joint. I could not walk on the leg, so I had to depend on a walker and someone to help me to the bathroom. At the age of thirty-seven, this was beyond depressing.

It was tough on me physically, emotionally, and spiritually. On top of everything, I was away from my dogs who always made my life so much better. I had to depend on my mom to help take care of them. Thanks Mom!

I won't lie, while in the hospital there were some days when all I could do was wallow. These were very dark times for me. I was alone, sad, depressed, and lost. I wanted to give up! "Why me, Lord?" I thought about all the wrong I had done in my life and wondered if God was punishing me. I had to believe that He wasn't, or I wouldn't have made it. I had to believe that He was giving me the opportunity I needed to develop my business plan. That is what helped me get through it.

6   https://www.merriam-webster.com/dictionary/MRSA

7   https://www.biomerieuxconnection.com/2019/11/19/
     mrsa-surgical-site-infections-what-you-should-know/

I pushed forward. On my strong days I kept working. From that hospital bed I spoke with both my banker and CPA. Tiki gave me hope. Hope that I could move on someday soon to live my purpose.

Once I was able to go home, I still had to spend a period of time non-weight-bearing and had a PICC line inserted to slowly distribute medicine to my body throughout the day. I had to be so careful in my healing process, but I still pushed forward in my goal. I still worked. I was ordering t-shirts and making final decisions on the marketing materials. When I could travel, my mom drove me to meet with the banker. I was exhausted and in pain, but I was inspired.

Since that time, I have had a second hip replacement, which is not the only unexpected health concern I have had to navigate since opening my businesses. The second time around, things were much easier in the recovery, however this time the biggest challenge I faced was being deserted by my staff and having to keep the business running.

I had surgery on a Friday morning. By Saturday morning I was working in my coffee shop. With the first hip replacement, I was not allowed to be full weight bearing for a couple of months to let the muscles and bone heal. The second hip replacement, I walked out of the hospital with a cane.

I remember slowly walking around the kitchen holding onto countertops. I was not quick but I was able to manage. Luckily, my coffee shop wasn't busy that weekend. In addition to working at the coffee shop, I also had to help with boarding dogs because of the staffing shortage. That first weekend was horrible. I remember waking up in the middle of the night alone and crying out loud in pain.

My poor dogs tried comforting me because they obviously knew something was wrong. Quick side note: dogs do make life better, I gotta tell ya! When you're sad or in pain, they will do their very best to make you feel better. Might be through a sloppy wet kiss to the face when you least expect it or a soft, quiet snuggle to let you know they'd take your pain away if they could.

In the end, I needed a bit more help than the love of my amazing dogs. I guess people can be pretty great too! One of my clients, who was also a good friend, would call me in the evenings when she knew I might be feeling lonely. My mother took care of me during the day, making sure I had food and helping me manage my daily routine.

Sadly, these two hip replacements are not the only surgeries I have had since starting my business. One day I was lifting a small dog crate while cleaning and suddenly heard a pop in my shoulder. A sharp pain immediately radiated down my arm. I tore my rotator cuff muscle with one small, simple action that shouldn't have been a problem.

Having to work for a couple of weeks with a sore shoulder until the surgery was difficult. Or at least that was what I thought at the time. Wow, was I wrong! The most difficult part of having a rotator cuff repair is the rehabilitation. For three months I had to sleep upright in my bed and had a huge sling on my arm that could not be removed. Talk about limited sleep and being expected to function as an entrepreneur! Now that was a challenge!

I think the funniest part of the situation—if there is one now that I look back—was the fact that even a grown man and business owner is sometimes forced to listen to his mom. I rested for a few days because my mother would not allow me to work. She was not taking *no* for an answer. She even instructed my staff to leave me alone. My staff was scared of my mom, so they didn't bother me at all. Talk about a needed vacation! A few days felt like two weeks in Jamaica.

But like a true entrepreneur, you can only keep me down for so long. That was something my mother knew too well. Of course, I was limited to what I could do with one arm. I was not allowed to drive for a couple of weeks. I had to depend on my mom to take me everywhere. I had a daily regimen of medications. It was all written and organized on a whiteboard hanging in my office. One good thing about being unable to work or move is being treated like a patient. I was treated to Mom's delicious salads, lasagna, and meatloaf.

Do your best to set yourself up for the times when you can't be there. Know who in your inner circle will step up in times of need.

Exercise 5.2
Reflection On a Cloudy Day

Connect back to your Blue Sky Moment for this exercise. Remember that big dream. Now, bring out your journal again and write about how a really tough time in your life prepared you to achieve this dream.

Take some time and write about the event without judgment. Let yourself feel all the feelings. Let it out. Cry. Scream. Put on one of your favorite songs and let it help you release. Again, it's probably good to do this in a place where you have some privacy and won't be interrupted. You don't want to feel judged. But it also may be wise to have the number of a good friend on hand if you need to talk when you're done. It is also okay if you write about an event that no longer brings out those kinds of emotions in you. Don't force it. Just tell a moment of your story.

After you've written about the event, reflect on how it changed your life. How did it shape you? How did it prepare you for future unexpected events?

Get specific! For example, what being forced out of my dad's home in college did:

1. It taught me how to work hard. By this I mean really hard! My life depended on it. There was no one else to bail me out financially. If I didn't work, I wouldn't eat. If I couldn't pay for school, I'd not achieve a life goal that was so important to me.

2. It taught me how to manage my time.

3. It made me tough. Quitting was not an option then and it is not an option now.

4. It forced me to grow up and take responsibility.

5. It reminded me that my life is important, my dreams are important, and that God has a higher plan for me.

Try not to be judgmental as you write. Let the thoughts and the words flow. You can always revisit and add or delete or edit. Sometimes you need to get an idea out so that you can build on it. Write freely and see what comes up for you.

I Don't Sleep

Emotionally, I am on a roller coaster most days. I can't remember what I ate for breakfast the previous day. The stress keeps me up every single night. I worry about paying the bills. I worry about hiring employees. I worry! Not only that, I also dream. I get creative. In these moments I am always reminded of the quote from Robert Frost: "I have miles to go before I sleep."

Sometimes it's during those quiet times that I am my most creative. I never stop dreaming up new ideas for businesses. This is what I live for, but sometimes it does get in the way of my sleeping. While I'd take the creative thoughts over the worried ones any day, one of the things I do to quiet my mind is keep a journal and a pen beside my bed at all times. This way, when I get an idea that really excites me, I write it down and release it so I can come back to it the next day. This helps my brain turn off.

That said, I maybe get five hours of sleep a night. Between the anxiety and the creativity, it is so difficult to keep my brain quiet. Why am I sharing this with you? Again, to be transparent. You can still run a thriving business and need sleeping pills. You can still run more than one business and experience crippling anxiety.

If you wait for yourself to be the perfect vision of what you think a successful entrepreneur should be to start, you never will. Just like me, you are an ongoing work in progress. While exhaustion is one of the expected challenges I face daily, I still find ways through it. Although there isn't a lot of time for self-care in my life right now, I do my best to take some time for me to simply just be.

Another thing I do to combat anxiety is learn. When I give myself the gift of knowledge, I feel good. I know I can do more. I know that in learning I become better; I become stronger. Learning also leads me to more creative thoughts. How can you worry when you're being creative?

If you need a great song to get you through some of the really tough days, I recommend "Survivor" by Destiny's Child.

Exercise 5.3
Combat Anxiety

Take a moment now and open up your journal. Write out some ways you can help yourself combat anxiety in the quiet times.

I'm Still Learning

When I started Tiki's Playhouse, I had this cool idea to provide luxurious private suites that people could rent for their dog. They were fancy! Each one had a really nice bed, a flat screen tv, and little doors and windows. Music was playing the whole time. I have to say they were really cute.

The problem was that they were expensive. People weren't willing to pay the price for them. It was a great concept but ended up being all wrong for the market, so I converted the kenneling area into a more traditional kennel.

That said, I always try to go for my big ideas when I can, and then when I need to, I scale back or get even more innovative.

Sadly though, some lessons I need to learn more than once. I have said and you will hear me say many times: have a year of personal savings to pay yourself and a year of capital in your business. This is so hard! But believe me, it is worth it.

When Covid hit I had not been following my own advice. I was not prepared. Luckily Tiki's could stay open, but the gym had to close for three months. I wouldn't have lost so much sleep if I had a year of capital to lean on. So trust me on that one, save the money during the good times so that you have it for the hard times.

Learn, Earn, Return

Learn more to earn more. When you earn more, you return more to your community. This is the best advice I can give you to prepare for the unexpected. The more you know, the more information you have available when you need it. You'll also have a diverse skill set to pull from when you have to think on your feet.

LEARN

Read books.
Take courses.
Get a mentor.
Network with other entrepreneurs.

EARN

Apply that new knowledge to your business and earn more. When I started Tiki's Playhouse, I didn't think about having a coffee shop in the dog daycare. But I learned how to think outside the box and developed a part of my business that allows me to not only create community but generate more revenue.

RETURN

Give back! If you have some lessons you know would help a new entrepreneur, write a book or offer a free online course. You could also offer to be a mentor to a college student with a dream. Think of ways that you would like to give back that inspire you.

When I am going through some of my toughest times, I lean into Deitrick Haddon's song, "Well Done". I strive every day for God to look down on me and say, "Well done, Kelvin. You are doing a great job. Keep going, Son."

I am not a very religious person, but I do have faith and that faith guides me. It doesn't matter if you don't believe in God, there is something guiding you to live in your highest purpose. A higher power. I believe everyone has a purpose in life. GOD has given all of us a path, it is up to us to find it.

Exercise 5.4
Clear Skies with a Chance of Clouds

This is the final part to the Blue Sky exercise you began at the start of the chapter. For this part of the exercise, go back and read your blue sky writing, and then your cloudy day writing. When you're ready, write about the following:

How will you use the strengths you've gained to set yourself up for the unexpected when living your big blue sky reality?

Quick Recap

The truth of the matter is that you will never be able to fully prepare for everything life throws your way. I mean, how many of you saw a two-year pandemic coming your way in 2019?

The only advice I can offer is to do your best to set yourself up for success when the rollercoaster is plummeting towards the earth.

Here are a few quick tips to remember during the good times. It might be a good idea to print these out and hang them where you can see them every day to remind you.

1. HAVE A YEAR OF CAPITAL! *I cannot stress this one enough.*

2. Have personal savings for the times when you cannot pay yourself.

3. Create open and honest relationships with your banker and landlord. *This one comes from the last chapter, but I think it's an important one to remember here.*

4. Do your research ahead of time. Prepare a list of resources you can fall back on when you need to.

5. Know how you will pivot if you can't pay your bills.

6. Constantly learn how to rob Peter to pay Paul. This means that you know what bills take top priority when there are lean times.

7. LEARN, EARN, RETURN! Never stop learning and never stop using that knowledge to give back to your community.

8. Remind yourself: YOU DON'T HAVE TO HAVE YOUR SHIT TOGETHER EVERY DAY! Keep going, keep growing, keep being the best you can be!

Chapter 6
Your Mom Doesn't Work Here!
How to Hire Employees

This chapter is all about people. As a new entrepreneur one of the things you will struggle with the most is not your product, it is your people! I have learned a lot about people over the years, and these lessons can be applied to your life whether you are already an entrepreneur or you are an employee who wants to be an entrepreneur one day. You may not see it now, but whether you are flipping burgers, serving drinks, or walking dogs for someone else's business, you are developing your habits as an entrepreneur.

So many people think things like:

"Why would I work hard for someone else's business?"

Or

"When I have my own business, I will give everything it takes. I will work so hard!"

Let me tell you, if you are not willing to work hard for someone else, you won't have what it takes to work hard for yourself when it really matters. Why? First of all, you won't have developed a mindset for giving it your all. David Goggins, a huge inspiration in both my professional and personal life, begins his top ten rules for life with: OUTWORK EVERYONE! He didn't say "outwork everyone only when it serves you." Outwork everyone because this is the best way to develop yourself. This is the only way to succeed![8]

Second of all, when you work hard for others, you are not only making money for yourself, you are helping another entrepreneur succeed. By being reliable, trustworthy, and dedicated to your work even if you feel it is beneath you, you also give someone else the opportunity to thrive. Trust me, it means the world to me when I have an employee I can depend on. I can spend energy on growth rather than the day-to-day needs of the business. Be that employee for someone else and you will recognize it in others when it is your turn to hire.

Not All Employees Are Bad

In my fifteen years as an employer, I have gone through good times and bad times. Every few years I hire a batch of good employees who stay with me for a while. I cannot tell you how grateful I am when this happens. My life is so much easier when I can trust that the people I am leaving responsibility with care about their work enough to show up on time and to give quality customer service.

I also love it when an employee walks through my door and shows an interest in being a business owner one day. This lights me up! I try to help educate and encourage all my employees, but it's so inspiring to share my knowledge with a young entrepreneur.

Growing up disadvantaged in many ways inspired me to strive to do something great in my life. My entrepreneurial spirit was born in those moments when I wanted more in my youth, when I hungered for more ease and less struggle.

---

8   Goggins, D. (2020). Can't hurt me: Master your mind and defy the odds
     - clean edition. Lioncrest Publishing.

At a young age I knew what it was to be an entrepreneur. I wasn't going to wait for opportunities to come my way, I was going to create them for myself. I am grateful for having learned this lesson early in life. So many kids today would be less entitled and ready to succeed in this world if their parents hadn't handed them everything. Do I wish my childhood was easier at times? Of course I do! What kid doesn't want the latest fashion trends or to have their college fully paid for by their parents? But in the end, I find gratitude in the strength my childhood gave me.

If more kids were inspired to go out and create opportunities for themselves rather than being handed everything, I believe this world would be a much better place. Take it from me, I have worked with a lot of kids and they have not been taught how to do some of the simplest tasks.

When I was young, we raked leaves, shoveled snow, cut grass, and even tried car washing. We did these things because we wanted to have what the other kids had. Although we lived in a predominantly minority neighborhood, we had white friends. I hated going over to my white friends' houses and seeing the "traditional family" atmosphere. Why were we different? Why did we have to walk everywhere? How come we didn't have our parents cheering on the sidelines at our games? Sure, there were times when my mom or dad would show up at our games, but why weren't they there all the time? I often wonder if I would have gotten a college scholarship if I had a better support system.

In our junior year, our dad bought my twin and I a Ford Pinto for five hundred bucks. It was a used mailman's truck. It wasn't a pretty car, but at least we stayed dry on the way to school. I bring up my childhood here for two reasons: I learned a lot and developed my resilience having to go out and create opportunities for myself, but I also wish I had more parental support growing up. I think there is a balance to be had, support your children in their dreams but let them work for it.

One thing I know is that my desire to want to help potential entrepreneurs goes back to wanting and needing that parental support I never truly got as a teenager. I remember writing in my high school senior yearbook something like "look for me in the NFL" not knowing what life had in store for me in college. I want to support the kids who work for me in ways that maybe their family is not able to.

The difficult part of this for me is that I get too emotional. I provide too much information, which often scares the weak. Maybe you've already felt this in the first five chapters. I am okay with that! I'm tired of the get-rich-quick scam happening in the business coaching world. They sell you on the idea that you can get rich quick if you invest in a high-ticket coaching package and follow their program. You need to know the truth, whether you are just about to hire employees or are an employee with a dream.

Sometimes when you read books by famous entrepreneurs—the ones who are millionaires and billionaires—you don't always get a good look at the tough stuff. I want to give people that. I want to give them a view of the day-to-day. The problem is that most people think they want to be an entrepreneur, but what they really want is to skip ahead to the part in the story when they've made it. When they have the big house and the fancy car and life seems easy breezy. That is not all there is to success.

You already know how I feel about that. Success for me lies in my ability to give back to others. Learn! Earn! Return! This is the knowledge I work so hard to instill in all my employees, regardless of their life goals. And it is so rewarding when I see them really listening and taking in the advice. I know they do this when they ask questions, when they show up early, when they go above and beyond with a client. People will surprise you in both good and bad ways when you let them.

Over the years I have had support from influential people, and in many ways it has allowed me to succeed. I can't say this enough: if it wasn't for my landlord, I would have failed years ago. For him to care about me and my business has been a blessing. He embodies what I mean by being a wealthy business owner. He gives back, and I have a duty to pay it forward.

Can you imagine what this world would be like if people paid it forward every single day? I mean truly paid it forward, in all the big and small ways. Buy some groceries for a neighbor in need. Offer a job to someone with no experience. Invite an old friend who just lost her husband over for dinner. So many people do this, but there are so many more who could.

You don't need three or four mansions. You don't need ten flashy cars. You don't need millions of dollars' worth of jewelry on your body. These things are luxuries, but they are not wealth. Wealth is how you are able to live your life each day. The opportunities you have to learn and to love and give back.

What do you think God would say at the pearly gates? Look around you. See the people in your family, your community, your country, and the world. You are a part of something larger. How are you contributing to the overall wealth of humanity?

Maybe a better question to ask would be: how could you waste the gift of wealth or talent on material things when there is so much good you could do in the world?

Wow! I went off on a bit of a rant there. If you just read it, it means my editor let me keep it. Now where was I? Oh yes, employees and my desire to pay it forward by helping prepare young minds for their own entrepreneurial journey. This leads me back to some of the lessons I have learned in hiring. Do you know what the most important one is? No matter how hard I try to always hire the best possible people, I will never get it one hundred percent right. Like I said earlier, I go through good times and bad times with my employees.

Ask any business owner and they will say the most difficult part of owning a business is employees. It's a catch-22 situation. A love-hate relationship if you will. Without employees you won't have a business, but sometimes the mess they make causes you more time and effort than they are worth.

That said, in any good business you will find that the backbone is the good employees. They are dedicated and have a true desire to see your business succeed. When this happens, you have found the pot of gold, however at times it can come at a cost. I have gone months without a paycheck to provide for my employees. It's only right. They are giving their time and energy to me, and I respect them by making sure they are always paid on time. One thing to always remember is: if you treat your employees with respect, the ones who care will do the same for you.

Have you ever walked into a business and everyone who works there seems grumpy? They get you your coffee begrudgingly. They are clearly waiting for their shift to be over so their life can begin. You might think to yourself something like: I guess that makes sense, this is just a minimum wage job to help them do what they really want. But then one day you go into a different coffee shop. You are greeted with a smile. The staff is happy and light. They are in a similar employment situation as the grumpy employees and yet they seem to want to be there. What is the difference between the two coffee shops? I would wager a guess that it is the ownership. When people feel respected and know they serve a purpose in their work, they will find joy in it whether it be playing with sweet pups, serving drinks, or getting your *double chai latte easy on the foam* just right.

Over the years I have learned that my employees are the backbone of my business, especially the great ones! Being who I am, I try to help them whenever I can. I have had employees call me to pick them up when they are stranded. I have lent them my own car in an emergency. I have provided paid vacations and paid sick leave, which is not something all small businesses can afford to do. I have bought food and clothing for employees going through a rough time and even helped them move.

There was a time when I would even grill some lunch for my staff on Friday afternoons as a way of saying "thank you for your hard work." Who doesn't like meat on the grill, right?! As we ate, I had the opportunity to conduct an informal meeting with the staff and get a feel for the temperature in the room. It was also a way to connect on a personal level with staff, not to always be *the boss*. In these moments we could just hangout.

I was unable to provide substantial raises, so I did whatever I could to show my appreciation and support. I would give free work shirts, cash bonuses when I could afford it, and offer opportunities to make additional money by working at night and during the holidays. I do this because it is right. When someone comes to work for you, I believe you have a duty to value their contribution to your business not only with payment but with respect and support. It lights me up when I have the opportunity to help my employees to grow and to get closer to their goals in life.

Finding The Right People

What I would suggest to any future business owner when it comes to hiring is simple: GET SOMEONE ELSE TO DO IT FOR YOU! I'm not kidding. If I could outsource my hiring process, I would do it in a heartbeat. When you first start out, you will have to do the hiring yourself, but pass along the job to someone else as soon as you can.

As a business owner, you will never find someone as dedicated as you are. You can't make someone want to be good at their job or care about their work. If you can separate yourself from the hiring process, you remove some of the emotional attachment you might develop when a potentially good employee disappoints you.

A few years after starting my business, I had to come to terms with the fact that I stink at interviewing. I always try to make it fun, which is WRONG. Do not do this! I have this desire to put the person at ease. I do this for a couple of reasons: the first being that I feel like I can get a better read on who they are as a person, and the second being that I don't like making people feel uncomfortable or nervous. I have tried to stop making interviews fun, but it is hard. I just go there instinctively. I can feel myself doing it, and for some reason I just keep running with it. But believe me when I tell you to keep the interview very professional.

If you start your relationship with an employee in a casual way, it diminishes the respect they will have for your authority in the future. As you can tell, I don't always play the part of boss and I do like to have good relationships with my employees. But I have learned the hard way that it is good to make sure they know who is boss in the moments when they need to. Especially if they have made a mistake or haven't been doing their job in the way that is expected of them.

That said, the most difficult thing I have to deal with is when an employee doesn't accept their downfalls. Everyone has faults; no one is perfect! But sometimes when you try to get someone to see and accept their faults, they dig their heels in. It can be hard to see where you fall short!

The old saying goes, "you can lead a horse to water, but you can't make him drink." In my experience as an employer, I have found this to be so true! I give every employee the opportunity to prove themselves and grow within my company. I offer my time for free. I give examples daily of how to do things that might help. And I keep them informed about my future plans as a business owner.

I include my employees in what is happening with the business in the hopes that it will help provide them with a stable environment where they can grow. I have even offered partnership, profit sharing, ownership, and the potential of renting to own. Some employees are keen to accept the opportunity at first, but in the end there is always a reason why they can't cut the mustard. Most of the time it's my fault, according to my employees. I push too hard. I guess it's better for them to fail with me than to try to start a business on their own. So in a way, although disappointing for me, my teaching did have some benefit for the learner. They know what they don't want to do in life!

Do I feel like I was taken advantage of by some employees? Yes! And you will too. This is just a normal part of the process, although it does hurt. You are human after all!

I can remember going above and beyond for several employees to help teach them about business. I spent years training and shaping and helping one in particular to grow their inner strength. But in the end they didn't have the stability to stand alone. Looking back, I can see what the problem is a lot of the time: helicopter parents! I touched on this a bit earlier, but if you know an employee has parents who do everything for them, they will have a bigger challenge in standing on their own in life. You can try, but be prepared to let go when they don't get it. Only put as much energy in as you feel you can spare. Here's the big thing to remember if you embark on trying to help an employee grow: let go of the outcome!

My fault is that I try to pay it forward to people who are not ready to grow. I still haven't learned how to be selective. Sometimes I think this is because I want to give everyone a chance without judgment, but in many ways I feel I still haven't learned my worth. I don't always see the value I have to share. This is a part of what this book is. It is me sharing my value with whoever wants to grab onto it and use it to grow. I come to you as a human being, an ongoing work in progress who is always evolving. If I were to write another book after being in business for twenty-five years, it would be something completely different. I share with you my honest and open experience because that is what will help you learn.

Should I be putting so much energy into my employees' needs? Should I care about them and their growth as much as I do? Sometimes I think yes and sometimes I think no. The one thing I hope I never do is turn off my desire to care about the people who walk through my door and depend on me for not only their income, but to help them learn. This person might be one in a million, but I want to be there when they are!

Don't Put the Poo In The Washer

Man-oh-man do I have some funny stories for you! The things some kids have never been taught at home blows my mind. It's infuriating to deal with at the time, but it always gives me and Uncle Willie a good laugh in the boardroom!

I mean, how does one not know to remove the poo from within the crumpled towel before they put it in the washer? Where do they think the poo goes? To magic washer heaven? NO…IT DOES NOT! It gets smeared everywhere, so you have to not only rewash the whole load, you have to clean the inside of the washer.

I run a dog daycare. There will be accidents on occasion, and I never ever thought I would have to ask a candidate if they would know to put the poo in the garbage before washing the towel. It's this story and others that prompted one of the best belly laughs I think I have experienced in the last fifteen years.

One night Uncle Willie and I were having a board meeting and grilling steaks on the deck. I was sipping on some of Uncle Nearest's finest and smoking a cigar. It was one of those rare moments of relaxation that are sometimes like unicorns flying over a pot of gold at the end of a rainbow.

I remember telling Uncle Willie how a new employee didn't know the difference between Windex and Pine-Sol. I mean, seriously?! If you were asked to clean a window and you had a choice between something named Windex and something named Pine-Sol, which would you choose? Maybe the one that has part of the word *window* right in its name?

Anyhow, I continued telling stories about some of the funny things employees had done that summer. We laughed so hard our stomachs were cramping. I know it may sound mean, but this was just the kind of relief I needed.

Another great story was about an employee who didn't know the difference between a vacuum and a mop. How? I just don't understand! How is this child of an age where they can legally work, and yet they have never seen an adult in their home use either a mop or a vacuum.

Another funny one was the employee who could not manage to wake up on time. EVER! Finally, rather than firing an employee who had some potential, I agreed to help them make it to work on time. When they woke up in the morning, they would text me to tell me they were up. If I didn't hear from them, I would call.

Okay, this next one is the funniest story! It's the last one, I promise. Or well, maybe not the funniest but the most mind blowing. The employee had no idea how to handle money, which maybe isn't that surprising nowadays. They couldn't figure out how to give someone their change. The cost of the latte was $3.25, and the customer gave them $4.00. Easy, right? Wrong, my friends! I had to step in and help. The answer is $0.75. Three quarters! REALLY!

These are just some of the stories I shared with Uncle Willie that evening. As our stomachs cramped from laughing so hard, the muscles in my face started to feel it too. In the moment we couldn't help ourselves from developing a fake job application for future questions that included questions like:

1. Who does your laundry?

2. Do you know how to do laundry?

3. Who wakes you up?

4. Do you know what color Windex is?

5. Do you know how to mop or vacuum?

Of course, I was blowing off steam and would never be so inappropriate with potential employees. Suffice it to say that sometimes you just gotta laugh or you'll end up crying!

My Interview Process Now

Honestly, I can still be a bit all over the place. Like with most things in life, I go with my gut! Sometimes this has brought me some of my best employees. For example, a client at the gym approached me about hiring his daughter. While I try to never hire children of clients because this can often be problematic, he was a really solid guy. I knew he worked hard. He was respectful and he was kind. I hired her without even an interview. To this day she has been my best employee and biggest success story. I'll talk a bit more about her later.

When I do manage to follow my own interview process, it looks a bit like this:

1. The formal interview.

2. I ask them to volunteer one hour of their time to see if the work is something they are even interested in doing.

3. If they like it, I then ask them to do a trial run.

What exactly is the trial run?

In Maryland I am legally allowed to pay someone for six hundred dollars' worth of contract labor before I have to hire them. So I hire the potential employee for a week or two to test out the fit. I have found in this process that at least sixty percent of those who make it to the trial do not work out. Most of the time it is because they think it entails something different. They do not realize that playing with puppies and picking up poo can get boring. They find it hard and want something more stimulating in the end.

I now look for employees who can be trusted to be there on time, make sure the dogs are cared for, are good with the customers, and generally care about not doing a bad job. I say it that way because I have learned to manage my expectations, although it is still hard sometimes. If you want to save yourself some major frustration, remember that no one will ever work as hard as you will. EVER!

The Scary Side of People

Over the years I have collected some stories about working with people that would make you cringe or run as far and as fast from being an employer as you possibly can. I won't go into all of them, but one in particular is just too crazy to leave out. It is proof that people can really pull it together in an interview and maybe even for the first few months of employment. You can't always beat yourself up for having poor judgment. Some people are really good actors, especially addicts.

Unfortunately, I hired a young woman who ended up struggling with alcoholism. Within a very short period of time, she developed a crush on me. I probably didn't help matters when I got a call from the police one night that she had been brought in on a DUI and had no one to go pick her up. I of course went.

Fast forward to a not-so-distant night in the future. The same girl is banging on my front door after an evening of drinking. I open the door just enough to ask her to leave. She tries pushing her way in the door and grabs onto my necklace. As I pushed the door closed, she broke it.

I yelled out to her that I was calling 911, to which she threatened to tell them a black man had tried to rape her. I still called. The dogs needed a walk and I was trapped inside. You see, I live at Tiki's. When I say that I live, eat, and breathe my business, I am not kidding. I literally do. Well, I guess except the eating part. I don't eat dog food.

Anyhow, when the police finally arrived, she was gone. I was sure she was hiding somewhere but they weren't about to look for her. I waited about twenty more minutes before trying to leave and sadly had to call the police again.

One other scary story I'll share had to do with an employee being negligent. Luckily the incident did not cost me thousands of dollars, but it could have! I sent an employee out to take a dog for a walk while their family was away. He was supposed to go three times that day, but after his morning walk, he fell asleep. It was bad enough that the dog didn't get the walk he should've. He also left the garage door open all day! I got a frantic call from the client whose neighbor had noticed it.

I had to go over that evening to check that everything was okay with the house and the dog, and to close the garage door. The employee was fired on the spot.

There was also the employee who would drink my vodka from the freezer and replace it with water. Never, ever do this! You will be caught! Since I live at work, my food is in the fridge and so inevitably some employees take it upon themselves to enjoy a can of soda or a sandwich.

When you become an employer, some of your employees stop seeing you as a human being. To them you are a paycheck, so they treat you and your space in the same way they might treat a five dollar bill they are about to spend on some useless thing they want at the moment. The trick is to not let it get you down. It's hard. When you have a big heart and treat others with respect, you would hope you would be treated the same way. Let it go. For some people you will always just be the paycheck until they move onto the next place.

Keep The Good Ones

I mentioned earlier that on top of payment, I try to offer some perks to not only keep my employees happy but to let them know that I am grateful for all they do. Things like discounts on the products and free gym memberships really help, but the best way to honor your employees' work is to pay them on time every time! I hold myself accountable to this!

I also try to provide a fun work environment. I know what it is like to dread going to work. I don't want my employees to feel that way. I want them to look forward to coming in. So I do the best I can to keep it light.

Another great way to keep the good employees—which I've also talked a lot about—is to share your knowledge with them. Give them all the opportunities you can to help them learn.

Keep your employees interested and engaged by telling them all about your future plans for the business. Listen to their ideas and let them get excited too. This doesn't mean you have to use their ideas. Let them feel heard and explain why you choose not to use an idea.

The bottom line is: when a good employee walks through your door, let them know that they are valued by paying them on time, allowing them to contribute to the business, and giving them opportunities to grow!

Quick Recap

1. If you can, get someone else to do your hiring for you.

2. Stay professional at all times.

3. Remember that you are the boss.

4. Manage your expectations.

5. Respect your staff and treat them well. If you do this, the good ones will stay.

Chapter 7
Glory Days
How To Define & Redefine Your Success

Just as I began writing this chapter, I was asked if I was a success. Without hesitation, I responded "no."

What?!

I know, I know. As a reader you might be confused, and I get that. I mean, there was a whole page where I outlined some of my successes with you. But you see, I am human and I waver on what success is and what it means to me. So yes, some days I know without a doubt that being in business for fifteen years after all the challenges I have faced in this life is a huge success.

But when I was asked that question the other day, I didn't feel that way. My current situation flashed before my eyes. I live, eat, and breathe my business. Is this success? At that moment, my gut response was NO. Why? Because I am ready to take my life and my business to the next level of success.

I have read so many books by entrepreneurs that have made billions. They live in big houses. They eat at the best restaurants. They wear expensive clothes. I love those books. They inspire me to look forward, to keep going, to plan what I like to call my *glory days*. What are the glory days? They are the days when I will be able to make breakfast at home. Breakfast is my favorite meal. And then I'll take a leisurely shower without worrying about getting to work because my employees are on it! I might go to the shooting range for a bit and then head in after. These are the glory days, when I can truly enjoy the fruits of my labor. This is the next level of my success.

Why am I writing this book now, at my current level of success? You already know the big reason: I felt called to give back. To return some knowledge to the world. But another big reason is because while the books by those who have already made it to the next level are great, I believe that more books by those of us still in the trenches are just as important. If you are already in business but haven't hit your glory days yet either, I am here walking alongside you. Let's do this together.

I am here to push you to your limits, to give you that extra edge you need to get you to your glory days. I grew up without privilege. I live my life now without privilege in a time when humanity needed to band together to abolish racism for good, rather than allow ourselves to be divided further. I want more books that highlight those of us who keep going, who keep doing, who keep fighting to create something that is theirs. I want this chapter to be the one you come back to again and again and again when you need that little extra edge to keep YOU going.

I write this now after getting knocked down hard by Covid and while facing a new kind of pandemic. Staff are harder and harder to come by these days. When I do find them, I have to pay a higher wage to retain them. Don't get me wrong, I want to pay people well, but lately I am having to sacrifice to stay competitive with my staff wages.

This is today, in the moment of writing this book near the end of 2022. This is where I am at. Here is how I keep my head up and work forward. I continue to LEARN, EARN, AND RETURN! In this chapter I am going to learn, earn, and return right alongside you. Together we will lift ourselves up into our glory days!

Remember This

Before I get into the meat of this chapter, I'm going to share a very important reminder with those of you who have not yet started your business. Use this reminder to guide you in the work you do in this chapter.

Here it is, the most important advice you will ever receive as a new entrepreneur:

FUCK THE BANKS!

Pardon my language, but seriously, do not take a loan. Start small. And I mean really small. Build an online business from your parents' basement, or from the tiny apartment you share with five other people—who you wish knew how to wash a dish. Or even from your car. Get creative!

START SMALL
START SMART!

MOVE SLOW
LEARN
GROW
INVEST

USE YOUR OWN MONEY!

If you have a really big idea, take some time now and think about how you can make it work in stages. You might be thinking, *"No way, Kelvin. I either go big or I go home."* Yes, for some this works, but just play devil's advocate with me here for a second. Is there a way you could work towards your idea, with a smaller idea, just to get it going without having to get a loan?

Think about Tiki's for example. One of the things I could've done was start by dog walking and pet sitting. Cross market the two businesses. I could have incorporated waste removal and taxi services. All of these services could have been done on a shoestring budget. Get creative with how to make money when starting out small. Think outside the box. Be the butterfly who leaves the box to be free.

Exercise 7.1
Reflect

One of the things I have done throughout my life is journal. And I keep every single one so that I can go back to them. There is such huge value in putting pen to paper. It allows you to get your ideas out so your brain can stop trying to hold onto them. It also allows you to record and recognize your milestones. Finally, it gives you the opportunity to be honest with yourself. Acknowledge the areas of your mindset that are holding you back and the knowledge or skills you are missing that would help you achieve your goals.

You don't have to journal every single day, or even every week. Sometimes I only journal once a month. Do it when it works for you or when you feel you need it. Like right now! As I've said, you'll get more from this book if you do the work as you are reading. So go get your journal and take a moment now to reflect on the following:

If success could be viewed in levels, what is your current level of success? For example, my current level of success is being in business for fifteen years, against some tough odds. If you aren't in business yet, you are still at a level of success. It could be anything from having a great idea, having many great ideas, to finishing a course for a college program. Write about your skills. Write about all the things that make you awesome.

Know Your Worth

Throughout this chapter I am going to continue to share with you some of the books that have given me that extra edge when I needed it. Within each section I'll share an exercise based on what I learned from the book. That said, I highly recommend you read these books and take from them what you need. Knowledge is a gift in itself. It is one you don't have to wait for anyone else to give you. It is out there in the world, ready for you to simply open up your mind, body, and spirit to receive.

Read

Book: *Bring Yourself: How to Harness the Power of Connection to Negotiate Fearlessly.*
Author: Mori Taheripour.

Negotiating! You do it more often than you think, and yet you probably think of it as a skill you don't already possess. Mori Taheripour offers some excellent insight into the art of negotiation, especially in the area of understanding your own worth. This was huge for me!

Taheripour talks a lot about the importance of bringing your authentic self to every negotiation. What does this mean? Remove the mask. Let the world see you. Easier said than done, right? I don't think so, but you have to put in the work to really get to know your authentic self and to understand the value you bring to the table.

The second lesson this book reminded me of is to ask for value in the services I pay for. Do not accept poor service! That is the bottom line. There are so many reasons we do this, but the main one connects back to not recognizing your own worth. So yes, you can expect your employees to do their job, and even to do it well! When you own who you are and allow your authentic self to come to each negotiation in life, people will see you and your worth.

Exercise 7.2
Reflect

Who are you? Without the mask. Write about yourself as if you are a charac-
ter in a book. Describe the real you.

Here is my response to the exercise to get you started:

You know me. I'm the guy who will drop what I am doing to help a friend or a neighbor or even a stranger in need. I value hard work and I don't just expect it from others. I work hard myself. I believe in giving back, even in times when you are struggling. I know, without a doubt, this path I am on is exactly the one the

Universe has created for me. I work every day to live in faith. I am strong. I am resilient. I do not quit!

This is just a start. Keep writing. Expand on all the good that you are and all the good you are working towards. This writing is not about dwelling on your perceived shortcomings. Build yourself up!

Now that you have begun to get really clear with yourself about who you are, it's time to own your worth. Decide. What are you worth right now? You can do some research with this to see what the going rate is for your service, but keep in mind that you get to decide your worth. Don't ever let anyone else define your worth for you.

Finally, write out a response to the following question:

Why should your customer pay you the amount you are charging?

Own Your Actions

"Extreme Ownership. Leaders must own everything
in their world. There is no one else to blame."

—Jocko Willink[9]

Read

Book: *Extreme Ownership: How U.S. Navy SEALs Lead and Win*
Authors: Jocko Willink and Leif Babin

There is so much value in this book! The one thing it taught me was to stay focused and to never, ever give up. It did so in a way you might not think of; it asked me to take ownership of my failures. It is so easy to blame external

---

9   Willink, Jocko , and Leif Babin. 2017. Extreme Ownership: How U.S. Navy SEALs Lead and Win. St. Martin's Press.

sources. I could easily quit, go back to having a stable nine to five job, and blame it on Covid, or the current staffing shortage, or the lack of privilege I've had in my life. I've got a million and one excuses I could blame my failure on.

So do you. Your challenges might be different from mine, or they might be similar. Maybe you grew up in a poor neighborhood without a stable family environment, or maybe your parents gave you everything but expect to be able to control your life. Maybe you found a great way to pivot during Covid that is now no longer relevant. Maybe, maybe, maybe…

Here is what I know: when I stop blaming the challenges of the external world and take control of my inner world, I am the only one who needs to take responsibility for every single decision I make. Every. Single. One.

You are the leader of your life. You and you alone. Not only that, you are the leader of the team you have working for you. As the leader you need to take responsibility for not only your actions, but those of your team as well. In *Extreme Ownership*, the reader learns about a common practice that happens during what they call Hell Week in Navy SEAL training. This particular week is meant to push the participants past their physical limits. If you want to talk about getting comfortable being uncomfortable, this week defines it!

Throughout this training there are regular boat races. There are two boats, each with six rowers and one leader. After a race, the teams switch leaders, making the winning leader move to the losing team. In every case, the team that wins switches. It is not about the team, it is about the leader. Be the leader in your life. Take ownership of all that you do and you will keep going, even when the water gets choppy.

Exercise 7.3
Reflect

In your last reflection you wrote about yourself and your worth. Do not let this next reflection diminish any of that. The fact that you make mistakes or need to strengthen some skills does not diminish your worth.

Of course, if you are new to a skill or a trade, you may charge less to reflect that. However, do not stay there for long. Always raise your prices to reflect the time, effort, and knowledge you have gained from your experiences.

That said, here are a few questions for you to reflect on:

1. What challenges am I currently facing that I am blaming for getting in my way?

2. How can I help myself face new challenges by gaining more strength and knowledge?

3. What excuses am I making for being less disciplined than I could be?

Make Your Bed

> "There are the occasional great men and women of science who changed history at an early age, but most discoveries, most achievements, most triumphs are the product of a long and painful process and only the most resolute, the ones that can persevere through the failure, the rejection, the ridicule, the emotional and physical strain of time—those are the ones most likely to save the world."
>
> —William H. McRaven[10]

That last quote was from an inspiring speech given by William H. McRaven at the MIT commencement address in May of 2020. A lot of what he says resonates deeply with me and with my message for you in this book. I wish I could print the whole thing here, but I am sure that would be a copyright

---

10 https://commencement.mit.edu/commencement-archive/2020/speakers/
admiral-william-h-mcraven

infringement, so I will share one more quote before I tell you why you should read his book next:

"It would be easy to stand up here and tell you that there is a wondrous place where you can be great at both work…and life, where your efforts to make a difference in the world come easy—but I have never found that place. In the end, if your goal is a noble one, then your sacrifice will be worth it. And you will be proud of what you have accomplished."[11]

I know my goal is without a doubt a noble one and this is why I sacrifice. This is why I live, eat, and breathe my business, so that one day I will be able to help others have an easier time of it. My lessons are your lessons, in the same way that if you choose to share your knowledge with the world, your lessons will be the lessons that help others achieve their entrepreneurial dreams with greater ease.

Read

Book: *Make Your Bed: Little Things That Can Change Your Life…and Maybe the World*
Author: William H. McRaven

I learned a valuable lesson from this book, and it is a simple one: wake up every single morning and make your bed. Why? Because it is an easy accomplishment to conquer. It's not just about throwing the blankets over and walking away. It's about taking a moment and doing it right. You don't have to do it with the same precision as McRaven did as a Navy SEAL, but make it neat and tidy and ready to crawl into at the end of a long day.

When you do this, you give yourself the gift of having achieved a goal at the start of each day. You have already done one thing right! This will help you, especially on the days when no matter how hard you try, everything you do is all wrong!

---

11   https://news.mit.edu/2020/william-mcraven-commencement-address-0529

In this book McRaven shares the commencement speech he gave at Harvard in 2014. He talked about how he had to face the uniform inspection in the six months of Navy SEAL training. More often than not, the inspectors would find something wrong. On these days he had to run out into the water with his full uniform on and then roll on the beach, covering himself in sand. He then would have to wear his dirty, wet uniform all day.

Those who ultimately didn't make it through the training began to feel bitter about how the instructors were so picky. They noticed all the little things that weren't right without acknowledging the care they had put into getting their uniform 99.9999% right. This right here is a reflection of the way the world can be a lot of the time. You can get almost all of it right, and that one thing you miss or get wrong will still bring on some heavy consequences. Will you be the one who complains about how unfair it is? Or will you remember your perfectly made bed and let it go?

This point brings me back to the idea of strength and resilience. It is a balancing act. Yes, you can train yourself to be strong, but without some reward you will break at some point. Seeing the accomplishment in the little things will put some strength in your bank for when you get knocked down later in the day! Give yourself that gift.

Exercise 7.4
Reflect

This one is quick and easy! Make a list of three things you do each day that you could pay more attention to. Make a commitment from this point on to be present in the moment every single day when you are completing these tasks. What do I mean by that? When you are completing the task, don't think about what you are going to do next or worry about this, that, or the other thing. Focus on getting the thing done right!

To help get you started on choosing your three, here are a few simple tasks I usually do daily:

1. Make my bed.

2. Do the dishes.

3. Brush my teeth.

4. Get dressed. *I know when we're busy and it doesn't matter, it's easy to just throw something on and get going. What if you were more intentional and decided to wear something that made you feel good about yourself that day?*

5. Walk the dogs. *This is a fun one. If you have a dog, how often do you find your brain wandering onto your ever-growing to-do list? Intentionally pull yourself into the moment and play. Enjoy the time you get to spend with your pup.*

Read, Reflect, Repeat

At this point you might be seeing a bit of a pattern to this chapter: read, reflect, repeat! I shared three of the many books that have inspired my journey not only as an entrepreneur, but also in life.

Exercise 7.5
Reflect

Now it is your turn! Take a moment now to think about a book that has really inspired you. Pull from it the one thing that has helped you grow. Write about that one thing and then reflect on it.

By now you might be able to see how I did that. Mori Taheripou's book *Bring Yourself: How to Harness the Power of Connection to Negotiate Fearlessly* inspired me to own my worth and to use this to charge prices for my services that reflect that. Jocko Willink and Leif Babin's book *Extreme Ownership: How U.S. Navy SEALs Lead and Win* reminded me to take ownership of my actions. I am not a victim to my circumstances. I have power over my life through the choices I make each day. Finally, William H. McRaven's book *Make Your Bed: Little Things That Can Change Your Life...and Maybe the World* reminded me to focus on the small wins. When I get things right, I celebrate it, because there will be so many times in the day when the world will only see when I get things wrong.

So, what books inspire you to do better, be better, and make the world a brighter place? Write about those and then share them with someone who could use some of that inspiration!

Quick Recap

1. Know what your level of success is right now. This will give you a good base to move forward from.

2. Know your worth. Do not undercut yourself when charging for your services or accepting services from your vendors.

3. Own your actions. Let go of the blame-and-shame game. You are the leader of your life. Act like it!

4. Reward yourself once in a while. You deserve it!

5. Read, reflect, repeat!

Chapter 8
Accountability & Mentorship
How To Help Yourself Stay Accountable

"Service to others is the rent you pay
for your room here on earth."

–Muhammad Ali[12]

This chapter is all about asking for help, allowing yourself to receive the help that is offered, and giving help to others in return. By now you know I'm all about the energy of giving back. Learn, earn, return!

In my life I have had the opportunity to help others and have also had to lean on others when I needed help. This is the nature of being human, and it extends to who you are as an entrepreneur. I lean on others for their knowledge, their support, their understanding, and their perspective. I hope that others know they can lean on me for the same.

Mentors show up in your life when you least expect it, but you have to be open to seeing them. There have been times when I've looked back and realized that a person came into my life when I needed them most. Maybe I didn't notice it at the time, but they helped me. Mentors can also come in different ways. Sometimes they provide an example for you to model yourself after. Sometimes they are your teachers or your bosses or even your friends.

---

12 Muhammad Ali Quotes. BrainyQuote.com, BrainyMedia Inc, 2023. https://www.brainyquote.com/quotes/muhammad_ali_136676, accessed May 11, 2023.

Look out at the world around you. Who in your life is a mentor? Who can you lean on in times of need? Who can you turn to for more knowledge? Who do you model yourself after? If you are to succeed as an entrepreneur, you cannot be a one man show. Consider your business a newborn baby. They often say it takes a village! Find your village!

Get Accountable!

Before I share some of the ways people have had a positive impact in my life. Take a moment now and ask yourself the following:

Do I have anyone in my life who keeps me accountable?

When I say accountable, I mean that you have someone who calls you out on your crap. They don't let you hide behind your excuses. They remind you what your dreams are. They push you to do the things you say you are going to do. They question you when they think you are missing a step in the process or being too easy on yourself. Go back to that question again. Most likely, if you're being honest with yourself, the answer is no. Sure, you might have that friend who will call you out once in a while, but they aren't directly committed to the cause. In the end, if you fail they might help you get back on your feet or be there for you as you nurse your ego, but they have no real investment in the game.

Sometimes it helps to reach out to someone who is attempting to achieve a similar goal as you are and offer to be an accountability partner. This means that you both agree to actively help each other stay on track. You cheer each other on, help each other see when more knowledge is required, celebrate each other's wins, and call each other out when things aren't getting done.

Do you have someone in your life who could be your accountability partner?

Good accountability partners can be hard to find. You don't want to ask your buddy from college who you have beers with once in a while because it'll probably turn into the occasional fun night out. Don't get me wrong, I love a fun night out with friends, but it doesn't work for accountability. You need someone who will spend some time every week or two and get down to business. Literally! Do the work!

A good accountability partner might be someone else in your community who is a new entrepreneur or a fellow student who is serious about creating their own first business. If you don't know anyone, try to look up some networking events in your area or even online. You don't have to be able to meet in person. But you do need to be able to find time either once a week or once every two weeks to meet to discuss goals, actions taken, and progress.

Make a commitment to find an accountability partner if you don't already have one. If you've already tried it and it's not for you, I get it. But one thing I've seen and seen often is that even motivated people fail if they can't keep themselves accountable to their goals, especially when they experience failures!

Get Mentored!

I have been lucky in my life to have found some really great mentors. A lot of times they come to you when you aren't even looking. Take a moment and think about who you have in your life that might be a mentor.

One of the greatest mentors I've had in my lifetime is my Uncle Willie. I've mentioned him a few times now, and I'm sure that by now you know he is not my uncle. Uncle Willie is that guy who would do anything for me. He keeps me accountable. He gives me a hard time. He laughs with me. He calls me out on my bullshit. But most of all, he lifts me up. He helps me see the true nature of who I am when I can't see it myself. I can't even count the number of times he has sat with me in the boardroom and said:

"Kelvin, I know it's hard for you to see right now but people love you. You have made it this far. Difficult days won't last for long. Go take a walk. Get away from it for a little while. Relax your brain. Just sit and have a board meeting. I've been where you are. Believe it or not, you are exactly where you're supposed to be."

I can't thank him enough for the number of times he has talked me off a ledge with these exact words. Don't worry, the ledge I'm talking about is a figurative one! Anyway, hearing someone you look up to say that you are exactly where you need to be is invaluable. It gives you that extra boost when you need it the most.

Uncle Willie is an incredible businessman. At seventy years old, he is still working the way he did in his thirties. I respect that! He has tenacity, a strong work ethic, and an unwavering desire to succeed. These are the things that drive me. Uncle Willie is not only the mentor I can trust to keep me accountable and lift me up, he is also the mentor I can model my actions after.

In his life, he saw some tough times. It was not always an easy road. He pushed hard to provide a better life for his family, but there was a time when he thought he would lose it all...until he sold his business to a big manufacturing company. Sometime later he was shopping and walked by his product on a shelf. He told me how good it felt to see something he had created out there in the world for people to enjoy. Such an incredible feeling. This inspires me. I can't wait for that moment when I walk by one of my products on a shelf!

Uncle Willie is generous with his lessons and his stories. Man, that guy makes me laugh, especially when I need to! When I'm standing on the edge of that dark cliff, Uncle Willie knows. He does little things like send me a joke via text, or emails me a ridiculous meme, or invites me out to lunch.

But sometimes when I'm standing on a cliff of my own making, he calls me out. He makes me accountable. He asks me to work harder. He reminds me that as an entrepreneur there is always room for improvement. We are never standing still. If you stand still, you stagnate! As I write this, I can hear his voice in my head saying, "What else have you got, Kelvin? What are you doing next?"

The other business mentor I am so grateful to have had in my life is my landlord. What?! Did you read that right?! Yes, yes you did. "Landlord" often brings out the image of the angry man or woman banging on your door demanding money when you're half a minute late on your rent. This is not my landlord! As I've already shared briefly with you, he is an incredibly generous and giving person, but not only that, he is a businessman extraordinaire!

He has worked with me so many times when I have hit financial bumps in the road. He values honesty and that is what I have always been with him. If I tell him where I am at and how I plan to move forward, he is lenient and kind. And I know that he is this way with all his tenants in the many buildings he owns. It is entrepreneurs like him who make this world not only better, but a kinder place.

Like Uncle Willie, my landlord is in his seventies and still works hard. He doesn't have to. I imagine he hasn't had to really work for years now. But he does. He takes pride in caring for his properties and his tenants. It's normal for me to look out my window and see him climbing up a ladder to fix something or picking up garbage. Every day he is out there in his "blue collar" clothes making sure things are done right, and I appreciate that.

Sometimes there is this misconception of entrepreneurs. When people think about the successful entrepreneur, they think about the person in their fancy clothes driving their fancy cars from their summer homes giving orders from on high. That is not the way it is for many of us. It is the joy of the work. Sure, many who make it can afford the finer things in life—and there is absolutely nothing wrong with that. But the entrepreneurs who I model myself after love the work too. It's not about arriving at the destination, it's about journeying onto one destination and then the next and then the next. It's about growth in the doing.

Within the first month and a half of Obama being elected president, during the housing crash I thought I would have to file for bankruptcy. I spoke with my landlord and he agreed to decrease my rent for a period of time and allowed me to pay it back in arrears. That helped with my bank loan. The bank recognized my landlord's willingness to support me and allowed me to refinance my loan, which decreased my monthly payments. I am convinced that one move saved my business.

I have countless stories of how my landlord has supported me and encouraged my growth. I remember when I approached him about expanding Tiki's Playhouse by adding a coffee shop. Without hesitation, he shared his excitement with me about the potential. My landlord really cares about his tenants and truly wants the best for all of them. In return, I always do my best to help my landlord anytime I see him doing manual labor like cutting down trees, picking up trash, or pulling up bushes. If you can find a landlord like this one, you will have given yourself a great gift. It is people like him who will stand with you in both the good times and the bad. They might even give your business a lifeline or two when you need it the most.

Get Supported!

What's the difference between someone who supports you and someone who mentors you? Someone who supports you could be the boss who gives you extra shifts when they know you're struggling to make ends meet, a friend who stays up late chatting when they know you need it, and sometimes it is a family member who is a shining light on a dark day.

So yeah, there are some gray areas. Sometimes Uncle Willie is a mentor who is also a friend and sometimes he is a friend who is also a mentor. I guess the way I look at it is this: a mentor is someone who has done what you are trying to do, has succeeded at it, is willing to share their knowledge regularly, and supports you in your growth. Does that make sense? Whereas a supporter is someone who supports your efforts in various ways without having done what you are aiming to do. Maybe a few stories will help!

I've already mentioned Boss Lady in an earlier chapter. As you already know, she was awesome. I'm not sure I would've survived college without her. Literally, I might have fallen asleep at the wheel had she not allowed me a room to catch naps at work before my shift. But she did so much more than that. By the way, her name is actually Kathy, but I knew she liked it when I called her Boss Lady.

Anyway, outside of her helping me by providing a place to sleep, inviting me to meetings where there would be food served, and giving me extra shifts when she could, Kathy always listened. She'd listen to me share idea after idea after idea. Sometimes she'd just shake her head and laugh, and sometimes she'd engage a little more with the ideas if she thought they had potential.

On the days when she could see I was close to giving up, she'd just look at me and say, "Hang in there, Kelvin, it'll get better."

Some days that's all I needed, someone to acknowledge my struggle and to offer a kind word. Find these people in your life. I know that on the darkest days it can be hard to hang in there. You've hung in there for so long, but if you keep going, if you keep pushing, if you don't give up, it really does get better.

The best piece of advice I can offer is to find your Boss Lady, or your Kathy, and listen. Sometimes support comes from places you least expect it, like a busy boss who has a lot on her plate and still notices when an employee is struggling in their personal life. When someone like this walks into your life, put your ego aside and accept help. If you're reading this, thank you, Kathy! You made life bearable on some unbearable days. I have always appreciated you and think back on my days working for you with fondness. I love you, Boss Lady!

Another great lady who helped me make it through college was one of my co-workers at the bar. She was always there for me when I needed to talk. I've mentioned her already. She's the friend who reminded me to go hug a tree when I was feeling overwhelmed or tired or anxious or like I was ready to give up. She reminded me that a tree could weather almost any storm when it had strong roots. She reminded me that I had strong roots. I had already weathered so many storms in my young life and I still stood strong.

We would sit for hours some nights after work talking about life and writing poetry. Her voice was one of those soft, soothing voices that was just so comforting. We'd finish work around two or three in the morning and then head to a diner. For the five years she was in my life, she really helped to center me.

So far I've talked with you about colleagues, bosses, and friends in this section on support, but I've left out one big one: family! As you know, growing up in my house held some very challenging times. My cousin Pam was instrumental in helping me get through some of the worst of it.

My parents had separated, and as kids often are in a divorce, my twin brother and I were caught in the middle. Our house was foreclosed on, and we had to live at a friend's house down the street during our senior year of high school. We are still friends to this day!

It was embarrassing and humiliating to be homeless and to have to depend on others, but Pam helped us get through it. I guess the "Board Meeting" really started with Pam. I know I've mentioned the boardroom a lot and I also know you don't know what I'm referring to yet. Don't worry. I've left it out on purpose. I'm saving the most important lesson for last.

As young teenagers, we didn't appreciate what Pam was doing because we were depressed and sad about losing our house—and in a way, our parents. As men today, now that we understand what she did, we have so much respect and admiration for her. Seriously! To take time away from her studies to spend with her smelly cousins must have been hard on Pam. But true to her nature, Pam has always been a family person. Pam's parents did a wonderful job raising their children. To my Aunt Gloria and Uncle Scottie, rest in peace.

During a particularly bad time, Dr. Pam—as she is called now—was at Princeton completing her master's degree. She'd come to get my brother and I. She knew what was happening and she wanted to make it easier. She'd take us, her "Road Dawgs", out to do something fun. There was this one time in particular that always makes me laugh. My brother or I had put on a lot of Brut, a super cheap cologne from the grocery store.

"Oh man. Who is that? You know you're supposed to walk into a soft spray of it, right? Not bathe in it! Someone open a window!"

She was one of my favorite cousins for sure. I learned a lot from Pam and her family, not just in their kindness, but also in how they lived their lives. When you've got the support of at least one family member, let it lift you up. Thank them and let them know how much they mean to you.

I've already told you about our summers with our family in the south and how much we didn't like being put to work, but I have to tell you, I learned a lot. These summers helped to define not only who I am as a man today, but a lot of my values. Work hard! Idle hands can do nothing but get into trouble. The lessons I learned during these summers continue to support me today. They remind me why I am doing what I am doing. Those memories call me back to my purpose when I feel like I've strayed from the path.

Work hard, Kelvin. Stay true to yourself.

There is one last family I want to tell you about before I move on. They were very similar to us in that they had three boys and their parents were entrepreneurs. I am still close with the boys to this day, and I still feel like their parents support me.

Growing up I saw the struggles they faced being African American and self-employed. I witnessed their perseverance and strength in the face of it all. Their dedication to providing a good life for their children made them incredible role models for how I wanted to live my own life. What I remember the most are the happy moments they shared with their family.

For them, happiness was being able to invite neighbors to their table, including us, to share a delicious meal. Sometimes it was simply chicken and bread or biscuits and gravy, but it didn't matter. The food was delicious, and the company was even better. There was so much laughter.

So you see, support comes in many different ways. Seek it out in your life and let it in. Some days it will be your life raft on turbulent waters. If there are days when you can't find the support you need, take the advice from my good friend and go hug a tree!

Get Inspired!

In this life you have a choice. You can let the dark pull you down, or let the light raise you up. Now, I know that not everything is black and white. Sometimes the negative is all consuming and you find it hard to see your way out. Here's the trick: don't beat yourself up on these days. Be kind to yourself. Cry. Scream. Let it go. And then look out into the world for inspiration.

You can look to one of your mentors. As you know, for me this is Uncle Willie and my landlord. Or you can call a friend or family member. Find someone to lean on to help you move forward rather than backwards on these days.

Sometimes you might even feel good taking inspiration from those people in your life that have achieved a level of success you can only dream of. I have been fortunate enough to know many, but one stands out as I'm writing this. An old client of mine owned forty-five Pizza Huts. Forty-five! But not only that. He also owned a lot of the buildings that they were in. Wow! Yes, this kind of success inspires me, even when it seems impossible. I sit and I imagine Tiki's Playhouse all over America. Happy pups socializing and playing, living happy lives.

The advice this client gave to me:

You have to be willing to grow and expand.

Seriously, the best advice you will ever hear. Don't stay stuck in an idea that isn't working. If you need to pivot, it doesn't mean you've failed. It means you're smart, agile, and resilient.

If you're reading this book and it is one of those days for you, I hope that I can either inspire, support, or mentor you.

Who am I as a mentor? I am tough. I expect a lot. I don't let you off the hook. I don't want to hear your excuses. So if what you need from this book in this moment is a mentor, ask yourself this:

1. How can I take one small step towards growth today?

2. How can I take a bigger step towards growth tomorrow?

3. If it's not growth I need, how can I pivot to move further towards my goal?

4. Do I know what my goal is?

5. Do I need to redefine my goal?

Take some time with these questions. When you are done, read your answers. Notice if there is any bullshit in there you can call yourself out on. Also take note of areas where you can push yourself further or are allowing excuses to hold you back. Go back and answer questions again and do the same reflection. Complete these steps until you have at least one action you can take. That action doesn't have to be huge. It can be looking into your next course. It could be researching your next product idea. Listen, learn, reflect, and take action.

Do you have a mentor you can reach out to? Do it now. Talk it through, then come back to your reading with renewed purpose and understanding. Give yourself the strength you need to persevere, my fellow entrepreneur. And if you still need some help, go hug a tree!

Quick Recap

1. Get a mentor!

2. Know who in your life is in your support network.

3. The people you love may not understand you. Manage your expectations now!

4. Find your inspiration.

Chapter 9
The Only Constant is Change
How To Embrace Change

"Change before you have to."

—Jack Welch[13]

The only constant you will experience in life and in business is change. Think back to the message I shared with you from *Who Moved My Cheese?* Sometimes you change because you have to and sometimes you change because you are inspired to. Either way, if you become complacent and comfortable, you will stagnate and so will your business. Yes, even the big businesses like McDonald's, Adidas, Amazon, Coca-Cola, and Pepsi are constantly reinventing themselves. If they didn't, they would die. It is that simple.

Take McDonald's for example. When you think of fast food, it is most likely one of the first restaurants that comes to mind. In 1987 they created the supersize option. People could pay a little more to add an extra-large fries and drink to their combo, but in 2004 things were changing. People were becoming more conscious of the rise of obesity and attributing it to the amount of fast food consumed by Americans. McDonald's had to shift again. They added salads and wraps to their menu to appeal to those who wanted to eat healthier.

---

13   Lowe, Janet. *Jack Welch Speaks: Wisdom from the World's Greatest Business Leader.* Canada: John Wiley & Sons, Inc. 1998

How about Amazon? It's common knowledge that it was originally intended to be an online marketplace for books, but since its humble beginnings it has become one of the most influential brands of our time. With a net worth in the billions, it has branched out far beyond its online "anything store" to include multiple subsidiaries, including Twitch (an online streaming platform), IMDb (an online database for film, television, and more), and Whole Foods Market (an upscale American supermarket chain).

Every company gets stagnant and needs to be revitalized. Technology changes, needs and desires change, and buying strategies change. After all, it's about making money. So you have to continue to keep your business new, fresh, and up to date. For example, if you have a website that has not been updated in ten years, you will have missed out on new advancements to things like search engine optimization.

The answer to everything in business is growth. Sure, you can maintain, but you won't grow. Do you want to be the hare or the tortoise? I know I want to be the hare. The quicker I get a jump start, the further down the road I will be. Sure, slow and steady can win the race, but does it pay the bills? I would rather reinvent myself every couple of years before the tortoise even comes close to catching up.

Throw Your Spaghetti

Have you ever thrown spaghetti at the wall to see if it's ready? It's a thing! Spaghetti that is ready to eat will stick. I love this as an analogy for business. It reminds you that some things will fail and that's okay. Just keep throwing your spaghetti at the wall until that one piece sticks!

There are always those moments in life when we push an idea aside.

"I can't right now, I don't have time."

"Everything feels so nice and easy right now, why rock the boat?"

"I don't think it'll work, so I won't try."

"It's a great idea, but I can't pull it off."

"It's not the right time, maybe when I have more of a financial cushion."

So many excuses. So many great ideas left without ever being explored. Sure, some ideas need to wait until the time is right, I get that. But sometimes you are allowing yourself to live in that excuse because it's easier to not take the risk. How do you know when this is happening? The honest answer here is that most of the time you won't. There will be those moments when you know without a doubt that something is right, like me with Tiki's Playhouse, but then there will be those times when you have to grab a plate of steaming hot spaghetti and throw it at the wall! Not every reinvention will work.

Whatever sticks, sticks. Keep throwing that plate of spaghetti against the wall until nothing falls to the floor. Be humble and know that you will have to keep picking up that plate. Be okay with throwing it from time to time. Throw it until your arm falls off and then switch arms. Think about Jeff Bezos again and how he started selling books from his garage. Now you can't drive down the street without seeing those ugly grey Prime vans. FedEx, UPS, and DHL have been around for years. Bezos didn't invent the wheel, he just kept changing the tires.

Take a moment and go back to the work you did in chapter five in the following exercise:

Exercise 9.1
ANTICIPATE CHANGE
Get ready for the cheese to move.

One of the best things you can do as an entrepreneur is set yourself up for success by having some new and creative ideas ready to go for when the cheese moves!

Write about one of your most outrageously creative ideas. One that you have never told anyone for fear that they may think you are crazy. Or maybe it's one you are so excited about that you've shared it and have been laughed at. It doesn't matter, write about it now with the confidence that you will do it.

Now take this idea and expand on it. Do some research to see if your outrageously creative idea has been done before. If it has, don't let that discourage you. How can you shine up that wheel in your own unique way?

Next, begin writing out a realistic and achievable business plan. Remember, each time your fear kicks in and tells you this is an impossible idea, kindly thank it for warning you and keep going. If you reach a problem that can't be solved, take some time and think about whether you've missed something or if there is another way. Maybe you could even begin this idea a little smaller to get it off the ground. Keep going, keep dreaming, keep writing!

If It's Not Broken, Fix It Anyway

Within the last fifteen years, I think the longest good stretch I experienced was approximately five years. I define "good" in that I was able to have a lot more free time. I was confident in my employees, and for the most part things were running smoothly. Did I still work on new ideas and new opportunities? Absolutely!

You might be wondering why. You've no doubt heard the idiom: *if it ain't broke, don't fix it.* Well, I disagree! Always look for ways to improve what you've created. And if that product or service has reached the peak of its performance, then add something new.

Even when things are going well in my business, I keep changing because there is always someone else who is hungrier! They will jump in and take your business, clients, or even staff away when you are busy being complacent.

Imagine if Michael Jordan, Kobe Bryant, or Tiger Woods settled when they won their first championship. They didn't strive to be better. They didn't practice harder. They let themselves stagnate. There are always another twenty or thirty Jordans, Bryants, and Woodses just behind them fighting to take that number one spot and hold it.

The difference between a champion and a competitor is night and day. A champion lives for as long as they are on top, they enjoy the moment of success. However, a competitor never rests. A competitor knows that if they rest for too long, someone else will gladly take their place. So a competitor thrives on being the best they can be whether they are the champion of the moment or working their way up.

Remember Mike Tyson? I talked a little about him earlier. That champ was fierce! A terror! But the minute he lost focus, he lost the title to a substandard fighter named Buster Douglas, who had nothing to lose.

A competitor realizes that a championship title is only good the moment it is won. Every day that competitor has to reinvest and continue to grow or they will be dethroned. Think of yourself as a competitor. Every day you must wake up knowing that if you get comfortable, Buster Douglas is around the corner waiting to take your title. So why should you reinvent yourself? Call Mike Tyson. He'll tell you why!

How often should you reinvent yourself? Hourly, daily, weekly, monthly, yearly? Maybe hourly, daily, and weekly in little ways. You need to plan for the bigger ways, but you'll feel if you're ready to do it monthly or you need a year. Honestly though, don't wait more than a year to try something new. Smell the air. Taste the water. Get a feel for your environment. If you are getting comfortable, it's time!

Get comfortable being uncomfortable. I can't say it enough! Everyday there is a new challenge. Everyday there is a new younger entrepreneur who wants to be the next Warren Buffet, Bill Gates, Elon Musk, or Mark Zuckerberg.

Learn to diversify. Learn to have many different streams of revenue so that you always stay on top. Even if you reach the top and are a champion in your field, you still want to be the ultimate competitor every single day. Why? Because the competitor is willing to accept new challenges not as a risk, but as a way of life. Competitors are never happy with just being champion. I don't want to be a champion; I want to be the ultimate competitor.

Kobe Bryant would show up two-to-three hours before a game and practice shooting and play the entire game in his mind before any of his teammates were awake. After every game, Kobe would stay for hours practicing and perfecting his craft. His teammates were champions, but Kobe was a competitor. All great competitors show up early and work late. All competitors work holidays, weekends, and birthdays. Champions rest, not competitors.

How do you stay competitive? What will you do to keep yourself learning and growing and being the best you can be at what you do? I bring you back to one very simple rule: LEARN, EARN, RETURN...REPEAT

How do you learn?

1. Take risks.

2. Fail. Get back up. Try again.

3. Hone your skills. Be like Kobe Bryant practicing two-to-three hours before the game.

4. Take a course.

5. Read more books.

6. Follow a mentor.

Earn

1. Use what you've learned to make some cash!

2. If you're not making enough to sustain or grow your business, don't bury your head in the sand. Learn more! Figure it out.

Return!

1. Give back. Even before you feel ready. Make it a part of who you are and it will never be the thing at the bottom of your to-do list that doesn't get done.

2. When you give back to the community, in a way you create a cycle of good. Those you give back to will give back to others. Goodness grows and will serve to make your community a better place, bringing more wealth and abundance to those who are a part of it.

Oh yeah, there's a few more parts to this:

1. Be tenacious.

2. Work hard! Seriously…work hard!

3. And never, ever get comfortable!

When The Spaghetti Falls

So you worked hard. You fought your fear. You pushed yourself to keep going. You earned, you learned, and you returned. And…then those few pieces of spaghetti that had originally stuck to the wall began slowly peeling off the wall and falling to the floor.

Sometimes you do everything you should. You put in the work. You're tenacious. You do your research. You get there before anyone else and are the most prepared. And you still fail.

A competitor opens its doors on the next block, taking away some of your customers. A national emergency forces you to shut your doors. You go through a period of time when you can't find a good set of employees you can trust. You suffer an unexpected illness. There are any number of challenges you will face that could threaten to take you out of business if you let them. Are you going to?

I have suffered many setbacks along this crazy journey, but I keep on going. Not every reinvention will work. About eight years after I started Tiki's Playhouse, I decided to open Maryland's first ice cream truck for dogs. It was an exciting time. I was really proud of this idea.

The concept came about when I started selling ice cream for dogs at my shop for nap time treats. Something clicked inside and I started researching ice cream trucks for dogs. BINGO! A new Idea was born. It's just that simple. Think of something not being done and run with it before someone else does. You are not reinventing the wheel, just adding some flare to it. Ask yourself this: if not you, then who?

I knew that the ice cream truck idea was a good one. If I didn't run with it, someone else would one day. So I went all in and suddenly I was asked to be on three different television stations and was featured in two local magazines. The first year was amazing! I was so busy I could hardly keep up with the demand. It was such an incredible feeling, the high of the success. If I am addicted to anything in life, it may actually be moments just like this one

That said, I made a big rookie mistake that first year. Every event I attended required me to pay a booth fee. The event coordinators charged anywhere between two-hundred and three-hundred-and-fifty dollars for me to park my truck at the event. After I paid that fee, as well as the cost of the ice cream and other products I sold, there was barely any profit left. There had to be another way. I wasn't willing to give up on the idea so quickly. There was so much hype. People loved it. I loved it! That was it, that was my answer.

Rather than paying a booth fee to the organizers, I approached them with an appearance fee of one-hundred-and-fifty dollars. I argued that I was a featured attraction, and since I would draw customers to them, they should pay me. It worked. Sure, some of the calls to be a part of these events decreased, but I was making money. If I have one regret, it's that I hadn't thought of it from the beginning.

Another great idea I had was to connect with a local liquor store and offer a puppy happy hour once a month. Don't worry, it wasn't the dogs who were drinking! The owner of the liquor store allowed me to park my truck in his lot without a fee. I'd listen to some tunes and sell my ice cream. It was always busy because it was always hot, and everyone had dogs! Of course, I didn't charge him my normal appearance fee. I made a lot of money!

One of the best things about the ice cream truck was that it gave me the opportunity to also promote my daycare and boarding services. I really enjoyed managing it for those few years, but as you know, what goes up must come down! I began experiencing a shortage of employees and had to make a choice to stop going out in the truck because I just couldn't manage everything. I was sad to let it go. Who knows, maybe I'll bring it back one day.

Another area I expanded into was grooming. It had never been a part of my original business plan, but I started to get calls and walk-ins inquiring about it. At the time we had a self-washing room that cost fifteen dollars, but it was always left in such a bad state that I got tired of cleaning up after people. The grooming idea was looking more and more appealing. I spoke with my landlord, and we did a mini renovation to make a five-hundred-square-feet grooming room.

The road was bumpy at first, but we started making money. Sadly, just like with the truck, the bubble burst after a few years, just in a different way. My groomer expected me to give them fifty percent, pay their taxes, buy their tools, and maintain the upkeep of the grooming shop. Oh, and they wanted to leave when the work was done and not wait for clients to pick up their dogs. I have found that most independent groomers charge way too much for their services and lack basic business understanding. I know there are some out there who are great at what they do and charge a reasonable rate. Unfortunately, I was not able to find one to work in my business.

Letting go of the grooming side of my business lead to me reinventing another aspect of myself yet again. On the day I decided I just couldn't deal with the drama anymore, I got in my car and took a drive, like I often do when I need an idea. As I drive, I look out at my community and think about what it needs. BAM! A gourmet coffee shop was born.

Turkeys Don't Fly

If you want to fly, you can't be a turkey! If you want to succeed, you gotta fly!

When I first wrote my business plan, I hadn't intended to start dog walking and in-home pet sitting until the five-year mark in my business, but I ended up starting both services after only two years because I was getting a lot of inquiries. I ran with it! Sometimes shit happens when you least expect it. I like making money, so I said, *"why not?"*

Was I ready? No! But opportunities don't come twice. Get comfortable being uncomfortable! At first it was hectic until I figured things out. Sure, I was running around like a chicken with its head cut off, but I was making money. On the days when I thought I couldn't keep going, I reminded myself to suck it up! Eventually I would take dogs that were not suitable for daycare or cageless boarding and do pet sitting in their homes. I developed a great name in the community and suddenly I was walking five-to-six dogs per day and pet sitting in the evenings. At my peak I was earning an additional $18K a year for these services alone. I was doing it all!

Another reinvention and renovation, which I hinted at earlier, occurred around year ten. K-9 and Coffee was born! This has been another labor of love. I'm so proud of the work I have done and the success I have seen with this initiative. The staffing issues, especially once I was able to reopen after the shutdowns, have been demoralizing at times. There was also a period of time where people didn't want to go inside, so I'd run out and meet them with their order in the parking lot. This didn't last long though. Drive-through windows, ordering online for easy pick-up, Grub Hub, and all the food delivery services has ripped a big hole in my coffee business, so I pivoted. It's only been a few months, but things are looking promising.

Welcome to K-9 & Coffee Lounge. Dogs, coffee, and booze! What more could you want, right? Food! Don't worry, I've got you covered. I also rent out a space on the property for a food truck. My latest investment in myself and my business was in applying for an alcohol license for the coffee shop. Reinvesting in your business is a must! Don't get comfortable. Remember, turkeys don't fly. Soar with the Eagles (Tiger Woods, Michael Jordan, Kobe

Bryant, Jeff Bezos, Bill Gates). My journey will not be yours, but every business suffers setbacks. Be ready or be ready to close your doors.

Be Afraid, Do It Anyway

Most people fail because they give into their fear. I learned how to survive at a very young age. One of the things my childhood taught me was to fight for my own success. I taught myself how to cook by watching people and experimenting.

You have to be afraid of something to push you to succeed. You have to be willing to make the ultimate sacrifice. What do I mean by the ultimate sacrifice? It can be different at times. Today I am writing this book on Christmas Day alone while family and friends enjoy the holiday. Clients expect a certain level of commitment when they leave their dogs in my care. I take my responsibilities very seriously at great cost to my personal relationships.

It's what people don't see that makes the difference. Don't let them see you sweat. Smile when everything inside you hurts. Give the best service you can no matter if people recognize it or not. Accept the bad with the good. Sacrifice for your employees so they can spend time with their families. I have spent every holiday and birthday working. Not because I wanted to, but because it was expected of me. Clients don't care about you; they care about the results. And the results pay the bills. Period.

Why do I reinvest in me? Because if I don't, who else will? You have to be willing to make the ultimate sacrifice. Your social life, family life, fun life will be tested. If you are not willing to be isolated for periods at a time, change course. All successful people will tell you that you must be willing to sacrifice in order to succeed. It's painful. Lonely. Depressing. Humiliating. Humbling. It's knowing what you are giving up and seeing no benefits, rewards, or monetary compensation for it in the beginning, and maybe even in times throughout as your business faces challenges. How long can you survive without a paycheck or without some of the comforts in life that you are used to? Now multiply that amount of time by three.

This is why reinventing and investing in yourself and your business is so important. This will help you get ahead of the challenges. You must constantly improve so you can meet the current demands of the market. Change so you can still be relevant. iPhones change yearly. There is a new social media craze monthly. The instant gratification fades fast with this generation. It's all about how quickly you can provide the latest thing. Covid taught people that anything could be delivered to their door. How fast can you get it to them?

So like it or not, businesses have to transform to suit the new generation. I have struggled with this for years and still struggle. I have not yet learned how to deal with the new generation. I never thought I would find myself thinking I was old school. Change with the times or get used to being normal. That word "normal" as an entrepreneur shouldn't be in your vocabulary. Nothing about your day is normal.

I can't help but think about Hem and Haw (*Who Moved The Cheese?*). The characters got used to the cheese and took it for granted. However, Sniff and Scurry knew change happened and they prepared by constantly searching for new cheese. Who are you most like? If it's Hem and Haw, change course now before you waste your time, and more importantly your money.

Quick Recap

1. Learn

2. Earn

3. Return

4. Never let yourself or your business stagnate.

Chapter 10
The Boardroom
How To Reflect & Grow

What do you think of when you read the word *boardroom*? Maybe an image of one of those big rooms in a fancy office tower with a massive wood table and leather chairs, where people in fancy suits give important presentations. For me, the boardroom can be anything. It can be a dock overlooking a serene lake at sunset. It can be my car as I drive around seeking new ideas. It can be a good friend's backyard. It can be my own office late at night while the pups are softly sleeping.

"What do you mean, Kelvin?" you might ask, "I thought a boardroom was a place where serious business happens?"

Oh, it is! But for me there are no confines in terms of the space in which this important business takes place. There is just one rule: when I enter the boardroom, I am creating space for myself. Space to unwind. Space to reflect. Space to grow. But most importantly, space to understand myself, my life, and my purpose. Space to be me. Kelvin. The man behind the business. The boy behind the childhood that helped shaped him.

I know now that I have been creative all my life, but I was too weak to see it. I was emotionally damaged by what was happening in my family life. The summers away from home. The divorce. My father's affair. The foreclosure of our family home. Living on welfare. Being homeless. Sleeping in my car. Sleeping in the library at Rutgers, too tired to drive home after a long shift. Stealing food in the hospital for dinner or lunch because I was hungry.

Riding my bike in all kinds of weather to get to work. Driving an unregistered vehicle to turn in a paper. Making a can of tuna and a bagel last for an entire day's worth of meals. Deciding that ramen noodles, tuna, pasta, mac and cheese, fish & grits, potatoes, chicken, and rice could all be gourmet meals if I simply decided they were.

All of these big and small moments are a part of what makes me who I am today. Some of it good, some of it bad, and some of it downright terrible. But this is me. This is my life and my story. The boardroom is a special place where I go to relive my life. Diagnose my life. Digest my life. The boardroom is therapeutic in many ways. It is a place where I work through, or simply live in, my emotional struggles. The hurt. The pain. The loss. The guilt. The resentment.

The boardroom is also my space to breathe and internalize my experiences. I visualize my future. I visualize my happiness. I visualize my life. I visualize women being attracted to me. I visualize being happy again. I visualize the hatred in my life being over. I visualize me being me. I dream about the places I will go. The things I will do. The adventures I will have. The trips I will take. The places I will eat. The places I will shop. I visualize a quiet comfortable life in Florida. I visualize being a humanitarian.

The Healing Place

Throughout this book I have shared stories from my life. I've gone into as much detail as I thought you would need to learn. My hope is that the experiences and knowledge I have shared will help you build a strong business right out the gate! But I also want you to remember that you are human, and all of who you are, as that human will show up in your business.

A lot of what I have shared with you—and much of what I haven't—helped to develop the entrepreneur I am today. As I continue on this journey, I have realized the importance of ongoing healing. The more you heal, the stronger you become, the more you can give to your business.

Healing is an ongoing process. Each day you do the work, and your own personal boardroom is a great place for that. Remember that your boardroom is not one physical place. It can be anywhere you need it to be. If you need to go out and sit underneath a tree, or close the door to your bedroom and let everyone know you need to be alone, or go for a run along the water. Whatever your boardroom is, it doesn't matter. As long as it is a place where you are comfortable being you in those quiet moments.

One of the last things I will do is hopefully inspire you to either begin or continue on your healing journey. You have done a lot of work in this book to become a stronger, more flexible, and even more creative entrepreneur. All these things are important, but healing is the quiet strength beneath it all. Let yourself cry. Let yourself get angry. Go to the boardroom and let it all out.

The energy of staying stuck in your hurt, your grief, your loss, your disappointments, and your anger is stagnation. It creeps in and kills your creativity, your drive, and your ability to see the good. Healing is a form of letting go, because in healing you free yourself to move forward with confidence and courage.

Take a moment now to write out a few goals for yourself in your own healing journey. Start by creating space and time. Look at your schedule and make time within the next seven days to go to your boardroom. Do something that helps you heal in some way. These are the only instructions I can give you. I am not a therapist, and I will add that if you feel you would benefit from speaking to one then I highly recommend it. In the next section of this chapter, I am going to share some of the things I do to heal. I hope they help you on the days you need it most.

Breathe

On days that I am feeling alone and burned out, I sit. Some days I listen to inspiring music. Some days I read Bible verses or motivational quotes. I have shared several books and quotes throughout this book. It helps me focus and reset my internal flame. The flame will go out from time to time, so you must restart it by taking time to breathe!

One of the things you can do to calm your thoughts is focus on your breath. I know, I know. It is so much easier said than done. Keep in mind that I am not asking you to master the art of meditation. I am not even asking you to stop your brain from thinking. It's your brain's job to think. Sometimes it just needs a bit of a redirect in its thought patterns to bring you back on track, and that is exactly what breathing can do.

Take a moment when you need it, close your eyes, and just breathe. Bring your attention to your soft inhale and your slow exhale. Do this a few times before you open your eyes and move on with your day.

The Bible

I believe that my life has a higher purpose and that even my struggles serve that higher purpose in some way—even though I will admit that the last bit is a hard pill to swallow sometimes. If I hadn't gone through the childhood I did, I would not be the entrepreneur I am today. You would not be reading this book. And maybe I wouldn't even have had the impact I have on the world around me.

As you already know, the most important thing to me is giving back. As I have gotten older, I realize that life is about service. Those who have been given so much have a "service" duty to help others less fortunate. Your servant's towel must be bigger than your selfish desires. Muhammad Ali said it best: "Service to others is the rent you pay for your room here on earth."

Now, I have friends and family that will read this and say "Kelvin, you are full of shit!" As you also already know, I'm not a religious man, although I've always believed in God. My mom would be proud of my goal to serve others and make the world a better place, but my brothers would laugh. I guess in some ways my lifestyle doesn't always fit the stereotype of someone who might say that. I can hold my bourbon, and cursing is a regular part of my vocabulary.

They don't know the real Kelvin. I have changed. Spending thousands of nights alone and feeling the emotional pain from my past has taught me a lot. I did not have the greatest childhood, but I had a roof over my head while others didn't. I was able to put myself through college while others served their country because they didn't have any other options. The greatest honor is to serve your country! The second greatest honor is to serve others.

One of my favorite things about working in the physical therapy department with Boss Lady was seeing people at their worst and witnessing them get stronger through therapy. It's rewarding helping people get back on their feet. Every single human being on this planet needs a helping hand sometimes. I know I would not be where I am today if it wasn't for the generosity of a few people who have been in my corner. I owe it to them to pay it forward. I know that no matter what, at the end of the day we all need help.

Oftentimes I feel I am not worthy of being loved. Not worthy of being happy. Not worthy of having a normal life because of my current situation. I struggle daily with feeling good enough. I work so hard because I have to prove to others that I am worthy. I beat myself up daily because I am not happy with where I am. I have so much to offer, but I can't get out of my own way. I can't stop blaming other people or situations for my issues. It's easy to blame your parents for a fucked-up childhood. But the truth of the matter is: I am fucked up! I have been working on being a better person. I have consulted with mental health professionals and currently take anxiety and depression medication. I have taken the steps to be worthy. I want to get to heaven and feel the embrace of loving arms welcoming me home. I want to hear, "well done, Son. Well done!" Until that day, I have to fight my emotional demons.

Like I said, healing takes place in the boardroom. I pray that God gives me the strength to continue the fight. I know God has a plan for me and he won't forsake me. I have to stay the course and walk in faith. I can't rush the healing process.

Even if you don't believe in God or the Bible, some of these verses may help you too. I invite you to read them if it feels like the right thing for you.

Bible Verses:

Proverbs 3:5-6

Sometimes you need to let go and trust that God (or whatever higher power you believe in), has your back. Walk in faith and the Lord will provide. Release and let go.

Philippians 4:13

For me this verse means believing in God and his glory, which will guide me to the place I am supposed to be according to God. I allow my faith to be my strength.

Psalm 30:5

This verse reminds me that pain and sorrow will only last a night. The morning brings new opportunities if you have faith in the Lord.

A few more of my favorites are:

> *Jeremiah 29:11*
> *Isaiah 43:2*
> *Deuteronomy 31:6*

Books

Knowledge is power. It is your greatest asset. The more knowledge you have, the more powerful you become. Why? There are so many obvious and not so obvious reasons. Of course knowledge helps you do everything. When you know how to do something, you at least have a good starting place from which to grow.

You already know some of the books that have transformed my life, but I want to share them with you again as we draw closer to the end of this book. Here is my list of highly recommended books:

Relentless by Tim Grover
Can't Hurt Me by David Goggins
Lessons from a Third Grade Dropout by Rick Rigsby, Ph.D.
Who Moved The Cheese? by Spencer Johnson, M.D.
Bring Yourself by Mori Taheripour
Extreme Ownership by Jocko Willink and Leif Babin
Make Your Bed by William H. McRaven

Each one of these authors and their stories have helped me in different ways. Some give me knowledge. Some give me strength. Some keep me on my toes. Some inspire me to step out of my comfort zone again and again and again. Some help me heal. Find the books that do these things for you too. They can be your lifeline when you need it most. When your thoughts are racing, find a quiet place in the boardroom and open a book that will help you heal and grow.

Music

Music is incredibly transformative. Sit for a minute and think about some of your favorite songs and how they help you in times when you feel lost, alone, sad, or are grieving. Some of the songs that have a way of lifting my soul are:

Am I Wrong by Nico & Vinz
I Smile by Kirk Franklin
Never Would Have Made It by Marvin Sapp
Rise Up by Andra Day
The Greatest Love of All by George Benson
Well Done by Deitrick Haddon
I Need An Angel by Ruben Studdard

Chapter 11
The Ultimate Recap!

To end this book, I am pulling together a quick and dirty list of the highlights so that when you need a piece of information and can't remember where to find it, you can just come here and it will help.

Chapter 2
Create a Successful Business Plan

Do the work! It comes down to these three things:

One
IF YOU'RE NOT A NUMBERS PERSON, HIRE A NUMBERS PERSON.

You might be too young to have seen the movie this comes from, but I'm sure you've at least heard the saying: "If you build it they will come." As whimsical and dream-inducing as this sounds, you have to do a lot more than build.

I know a lot of creative people like me who do not want to deal with numbers. But the cold, hard reality is your business will not survive if you do not understand the numbers. You need to get real with yourself about how much you can actually make and how much it will cost you to make it.

Also, when you are presenting your numbers to potential investors, they will know if you do not understand the financial side of your business. This is not a "fake it until you make it" situation. Hire a CPA or a CA to help you.

Work with a small CPA company, one with maybe one to two employees. Their overhead might not be as high, and this could save you money. Don't be afraid to interview your CPA. They are seeking to come aboard your team so drill them. You are hiring them. Make sure they are a fit.

Prove that you have the knowledge to manage your money!

Two
GET A MENTOR

Seriously! I cannot stress the importance of this enough. Ed at SCORE made me want to quit, but he did right by me. He was tough. He made me angry. But he made me get it right. He gave me some of the tools that ensure my success.

Get a business mentor through SCORE! Another great thing about them is that many of the mentors have connections with bankers. If they do, they might be able to set you up to meet with them so that you can begin to understand the bank's process. Start building your network early. If your banker trusts your SCORE representative, things will go a lot smoother when it comes to getting a loan.

Three
HIRE A LOCAL MARKET ANALYSIS COMPANY

Find a local company for your market analysis. This is very important. Chances are your banker will know the market and if you get someone out of state, good luck getting a loan. Stay local. This will cost you $$$, but it becomes a part of your business plan. The company should package everything up nicely for you so that all you need to do is print it out and attach it to your business plan.

Chapter 3
Tips & Tricks for Owning Your Financial Situation

1. Remember that it gets better. You've got this! Keep going.

2. Know that failure happens. Without failure you won't succeed.

3. Learn from your mistakes and move forward.

4. When choosing a CPA, look for a small business rather than a larger one.

5. Your Three Year Pro Forma is important! Get it right and you won't regret it.

6. Save enough personally to not pay yourself for at least a year.

7. Go to at least three bankers before deciding.

8. Bring a lawyer and CPA with you to meet the banker.

9. Expect the unexpected, and have a cushion to pay for it.

10. Be transparent with your lenders and landlord if you hit hard times.

Questions to bring to your bank meetings:

1. Who determines the loan approval?

2. How many people are involved in the approval process?

   The more people, the more questions and information to provide. Attempt to find out if the underwriter/s are available to discuss your loan. More than likely the answer is no, but why not ask?

3. What are the terms of the loan?

4. Can I refinance in a few years? If so, what will the requirements be for refinancing?

Refinancing is important, especially if you have a higher interest than desired.

5. If I decide to pay the loan off early, is there an early termination fee?

6. Do I have to offer personal collateral to secure your loan? If so, what are the details?

7. After paying back a determined amount of money, can the collateral be released?

   Meaning, if you have paid back fifty percent of your bank loan, can all collateral be released? Try to get your personal collateral back as quickly as possible. The goal is to keep all the finances related to the business connected to the business and not your personal finances.

8. What would it take to apply for another loan if your business is in good standing?

   Try and secure the ability to get additional loans in the beginning. Why do this? If something like another pandemic hits, you have the ability to get additional capital if needed. If possible, get it in writing. This is why you need an attorney. The bank will protect themselves. Period. Get as much terminology in your favor before signing the loan documents. Yes, it will cost you in legal fees and don't forget you need a CPA to review the financial terms of the loan. Spend the money in the beginning and increase your odds.

Chapter 4
Lean Into Your Creativity!

It is your creativity that will help you find the answer you need.
It is your creativity that will inspire you to get uncomfortable.
It is your creativity that will inspire you to stay uncomfortable until you succeed.
It is your creativity that won't let you stay comfortable for long.

It is also your creativity that brings you the ultimate joy!
A joy that gets you up in the morning, ready and grateful for the day.
A joy that asks you to settle for nothing less than awesome.

In the end, it is your creativity that will see that you always have cheese!

Chapter 5
Learn, Earn, Return

This is the rule I live by. Learn more to earn more, when you earn more you return more to your community. This is the best advice I can give you to prepare for the unexpected. The more you know, the more information you have available to you in the moment. You'll also have a diverse skill set to pull from when you need to think on your feet.

LEARN

Read books.
Take courses.
Get a mentor.
Network with other entrepreneurs.

EARN

Apply that new knowledge to your business and earn more. When I started Tiki's Playhouse, I didn't think about having a coffee shop in the doggie daycare. But I learned how to think outside the box and developed a part of my business that allows me to not only create community but generate more revenue.

RETURN

Give back! If you have some lessons you know would help a new entrepreneur, write a book or offer a free online course. You could also offer to be a mentor to a college student with a dream. Think of ways that you would like to give back that inspire you.

Chapter 6
Keep The Good Ones

The bottom line is: when a good employee walks through your door, let them know that they are valued by paying them on time, allowing them to contribute to the business, and giving them opportunities to grow!

Chapter 9
Keep Growing, Keep Changing

How do you keep growing? By changing! Don't let yourself get too comfortable. Stay competitive. How do you do that? LEARN, EARN, RETURN....REPEAT!

How do you learn?

1. Take risks.

2. Fail. Get back up. Try again.

3. Hone your skills. Be like Kobe Bryant practicing two-to-three hours before the game.

4. Take a course.

5. Read more books.

6. Follow a mentor.

Earn

1. Use what you've learned to make some cash!

2. If you're not making enough to sustain or grow your business, don't bury your head in the sand. Learn more! Figure it out.

Return!

1. Give back. Even before you feel ready. Make it a part of who you are and it will never be something at the bottom of your to-do list that doesn't get done.

2. When you give back to the community, you create a cycle of good in a way. Those you give back to will give back to others. Goodness grows and will serve to make the community you are a part of a better place, bringing more wealth and abundance to those who are a part of it.

Get Uncomfortable or Change Course

I began this book by telling you that owning your own business will test your strength in all areas of your life. It will push you to the brink in ways you never thought possible. I asked you to consider this book to be both a dose of tough love and your loudest cheerleader. Now that you are at the end of it, I hope you feel both of these to be true.

I still come to you not as a guru or an expert or a millionaire. I come in service. Take my mistakes and learn from them. Take my resilience as inspiration. On the days when you feel so alone it hurts, know that there are others just like you, entrepreneurs who also know they are on the right path even on the days when it feels all wrong.

You are your source of strength. Keep going. Keep growing. Never stop learning. Allow yourself to feel the joy of giving back as much as you can. Hold onto your biggest dreams. But most of all, get comfortable being uncomfortable or change course!

THE BOARDROOM

Acknowledgements

I send a big, huge thank you out to Uncle Willie for being my biggest cheerleader and lunch buddy. You are the one person I can count on to help me with the dogs when I am short staffed, make me laugh on the days when I need it most, and give me honest advice even if I don't want to hear it. I appreciate you more than you know!

Printed in Canada